History

Baseball in Blue and Gray

Baseball in Blue and Gray

The National Pastime

during the Civil War

◆

GEORGE **B**. KIRSCH

PRINCETON UNIVERSITY PRESS

PRINCETON AND OXFORD

Copyright 2003 © by Princeton University Press
Published by Princeton University Press, 41 William Street,
Princeton, New Jersey 08540
In the United Kingdom: Princeton University Press, 3 Market Place,
Woodstock, Oxfordshire OX20 1SY
All Rights Reserved
Library of Congress Cataloging-in-Publication Data
Kirsch, George B.
Baseball in blue and gray : the national pastime during
the Civil War / George B. Kirsch.
p.cm.
Includes bibliogaphical references and index.
ISBN 0-691-05733-8 (cloth : alk. paper)
1. Baseball—United States—History—19th century. I. Title.
GV863.A1 K56 2003
796.357'0973'09034—dc21   2002069289
British Library Cataloging-in-Publication Data is available
This book has been composed in Goudy text with Zapf Dingbats
Printed on acid-free paper. ∞
www.pupress.princeton.edu
Printed in the United States of America
1 3 5 7 9 10 8 6 4 2

For Adam Lavitt Kirsch

◆

Contents

Preface

This book serves a double purpose. First, it presents a narrative and analysis of the growth and transformation of baseball in the United States during the Civil War. Second, it examines the relationship between the sport and American nationalism during that tumultuous time. Historians of early baseball (myself included) have paid only brief attention to the development of the game during the years between 1861 and 1865, viewing that period as merely a minor interlude between the rise of the modern version of the sport in the New York City region during the late 1850s and the remarkable spread of baseball across the country during the late 1860s. But a closer look at baseball's progress during the war years reveals several developments that proved to be critical for the game's postwar success. These include the spread of the New York City variety of the sport to Philadelphia and Boston, the advent of revised rules governing pitching, and especially the growth of commercialism, fostered by championship competition and other special events.

Baseball's long association with American nationalism predated the Civil War, and the war intensified that connection. In the late 1850s many of the first clubs adopted names with patriotic associations, such as Young America, Eagle, Empire, National, or Continental, while on a few occasions ladies presented the Stars and Stripes to the players in a ritual that signified female endorsement of the sport as a wholesome amusement. The war itself provided the greatest trial of American nationalism since the founding of the United States in the Revolution. As northern and southern soldiers slaughtered each other to decide the fate of the country, sporting civilians and military men engaged in a far more innocent contest to determine which version of early baseball, or even the English game of cricket, would be recognized as the national pastime for the republic. The struggle to keep the country united and the search for a sport that would bind Americans together converged during these years. As Union armies overcame the Confederate secession, the New York City version of baseball became the most popular bat and ball game in the United States, widely recognized as the national pastime. Both outcomes were expressions of American nationalism.

The Civil War's influence on baseball is literally the stuff of legend. And, like most legends, there is both more and less to it than at first meets the eye. The ordeal of the Union and the triumph of baseball have been linked in the American imagination first and foremost through the Doubleday-Cooperstown creation myth, which casts a Union general as the inventor of the game, and also through tales of soldiers playing ball in army camps as they awaited deadly encounters with the enemy, or in prison camps as they awaited release. Several sport historians have stressed the importance of those soldiers' matches for the instruction of novices and the promotion of the new sport in all regions after 1865. But while the emergence of the "little republic of baseball" did not entirely result from the struggle to preserve the American republic, their histories are interwoven.

The chapters that follow recount the story of baseball on the battle and home fronts during the Civil War, but here it is necessary to evaluate the creation myth that ties the origins of baseball directly to a Civil War hero. On December 30, 1907, Abraham G. Mills, the fourth president of professional baseball's National League, issued the final report of the special commission that had been charged with deciding the true origins of America's national pastime. Specifically, that august panel had investigated the question of whether baseball derived from the English schoolyard game of rounders, or whether it was a purely native product. Henry Chadwick, a prominent sportswriter for fifty years who was known in many quarters as the "father of baseball," argued for the rounders theory. He had played the game as a boy in England, before he emigrated with his parents to the United States, and after a half century of watching and promoting the rise of baseball, he was convinced that rounders and the young American sport were closely related because they shared essential principles. As he explained to the commission, which consisted of former ball players and officials, as well as two U.S. senators, both were "played by two opposing sides of contestants, on a special field of play, in which a ball was pitched or tossed to an opposing batsman, who endeavored to strike the ball out onto the field, far enough to admit his safely running the round of bases, so as to enable him to score a run to count in the game—the side scoring the most runs winning the game." Although Chadwick conceded that the two sports differed in "methods and details of play," he claimed that they were quite close in fundamental structure.

Albert G. Spalding, an American-born baseball star and sporting goods magnate, countered Chadwick's view, declaring that baseball was "of purely American origin and no other game or country has any right to claim its parentage." He recognized that rounders and baseball shared certain features, but he stressed the many differences in rules: for example, by the late 1880s the two sports had diverged in the size and shape of the fields (square versus diamond); the number of players on a side (eleven versus nine), innings in a match (two versus nine), and outs in an inning (eleven versus three); and the size and shape of the bats (smaller and flat in rounders) and the balls (smaller in rounders). Spalding argued that rounders was closer to cricket than to baseball, that it was never played in the United States, and that any similarity between rounders and the American national pastime was simply a coincidence. A patriot at heart, he could not believe that in 1840 "our national prejudices would permit us to look with favor, much less adopt any sport or game of an English flavor." Instead, he was convinced that baseball descended from the colonial game of "old cat" in which a player batted a ball and ran to one or more bases. According to him, "old cat" evolved into the townball matches that were popular on village holidays in many early nineteenth century American communities, and modern baseball was simply a modification of townball.

Underscoring the game's uniquely American origins, Spalding explicitly linked the origin of baseball with the legacy of the Civil War when he endorsed the testimony submitted to the Mills Commission by Abner Graves. According to Spalding, Graves recalled that as a boy and fellow playmate of Abner Doubleday at Green's Select School in Cooperstown, New York in 1839, he watched Doubleday outline a diamond-shaped baseball field with a stick in the dirt, and he later saw him pencil a diagram of the bases and a list of rules for his new game, which he named "Base Ball." No doubt what struck Spalding as particularly marvelous (and useful) about Graves's story was that Doubleday had subsequently served with distinction as a Union officer in the Civil War, rising to the rank of brevet major general. Doubleday had been captain of the Federal artillery unit that responded to the initial Confederate attack on Fort Sumter, South Carolina in April, 1861. He later commanded divisions at Antietam and Fredericksburg and became one of the lesser heroes at Gettysburg. When Spalding submitted Graves's recollections to the commission he underscored the Civil War connection: "It certainly appeals to an American's pride to have had the great national game of Base Ball created and named by a Major General in the United States Army."

The Mills Commission also weighed evidence concerning the founding of New York's Knickerbocker Base Ball Club in 1842 and its first written rules of 1845. John M. Ward, a star player for the Providence Grays and the New York Giants during the late nineteenth century, informed Spalding that several prominent Manhattan business and professional men had turned to the boys' game of baseball for exercise. "There was not a code of rules nor any written records of that game," he wrote, "and their only guide to the method of playing was their own recollection of the game as they themselves, when boys, had played it and the rules of the game in existence, which had come down, like folklore, from generation to generation of boys." Spalding forwarded Ward's letter to the commission, which also considered a statement by Duncan Curry, an original Knickerbocker, who testified that "a diagram, showing the ball field laid out substantially as it is today, was brought to the field one afternoon by a Mr. Wadsworth."

In the end, Mills himself chose among Chadwick's case for rounders, Spalding's and Graves's argument for Doubleday perfecting townball, and the Knickerbocker claim for their New York City version. While he did not feel that the American origins of baseball should be sustained simply on "patriotic ground," Mills did not find the rounders theory very persuasive. Instead, he endorsed Graves's story, while noting that it was possible to link the Doubleday and Knickerbocker diagrams of 1839 and 1845. He concluded: "First, that 'Base Ball' had its origins in the United States. Second, that the first scheme for playing it, according to the best evidence obtained to date, was devised by Abner Doubleday at Cooperstown, New York, in 1839." Conveniently, Mills had been a member of the honor guard when Doubleday's body lay in state at New York City Hall on January 30, 1893. In his conclusion to his Commission's report Mills speculated that "in the years to come, in view of the hundreds of thousands of people who are devoted to baseball, and the millions who will be, Abner Doubleday's fame will rest evenly, if not quite as much, upon the fact he was its inventor . . . as upon his brilliant and distinguished career as an officer in the Federal Army." Thus Spalding and Mills concocted a creation myth for baseball that connected the national pastime with the country's greatest ordeal. As historian Bruce Catton has observed, baseball's legends "are, in some ways, the most enduring part of the game. Baseball has even more of them than the Civil War, and its fans prize them highly." The Doubleday-Cooperstown myth became one that baseball shared with the fratricidal conflict.

Robert Henderson, Harold Seymour, and other scholars have since debunked the Doubleday-Cooperstown myth, which nonetheless remains powerful in the American imagination because of the efforts of Major League Baseball and the Hall of Fame in Cooperstown. For the record, however, one must acknowledge that research had proven that Abner Doubleday enrolled as a cadet at West Point in the fall of 1838 and that his family had moved away from Cooperstown the previous year. Although he may have played ball with Graves during his boyhood, in his published writings he never mentioned anything about his role in the creation of modern base-ball. Furthermore, Mills had known Doubleday ever since their service in the Civil War, but his friend had apparently never told him about his notable brainstorm in Cooperstown. Finally, Mills's verdict rested entirely on an octogenarian's recollection of an event that had occurred sixty-eight years earlier. There is further reason to question Graves's credibility. A few years after he told his tale to Spalding he shot his wife to death, apparently because of mental illness, and he spent his final days in an institution for the criminally insane.

Modern baseball evolved from earlier bat and ball games during the 1840s and 1850s, and the conflict between the North and South between 1861 and 1865 severely challenged the new sport just as it was beginning to spread beyond the northeastern cities and towns that nurtured it during its infancy. As the ultimate test and crucible of American nationalism, the war initially retarded the game's growth, but ultimately it promoted the regional and cultural diffusion of baseball across the nation. The war diminished but did not destroy the excitement for the new game that swept through northeastern cities during those years, especially in the New York City region and in Philadelphia. Contests played on both the home front and the battlefront provided common experiences for soldiers and civilians, as the games in both locales boosted both the soldiers' morale and the spirits of civilians in northern communities. After the war baseball helped to bind all regions together even as it intensi-fied racial inequalities and divisions between African Americans and whites. The national emergency revealed and altered community, regional, and national identities in both politics and in baseball.

Over the years that I worked on this and previous baseball projects I have been blessed with love and support from my family and friends. I pay a special tribute to the memory of my parents, Anne Rizack Kirsch and Nathan S. Kirsch. They gave me the love, care, and support that enabled me to pursue a career in education, and their passion for learning and reading was one of their greatest gifts to me. I thank my brother, Daniel Kirsch, his wife, Laura, and their daughters Jennifer, Gabrielle, and Elissa for their encouragement. I must single out Elissa in particular for some long and mostly fruitless hours of research for me in the Boston Public Library. I also appreciate the decades of friendship and sportsmanship shared with Kevin Clermont, Barry Cohen, Henry Cenicola, Richard Prager, Barry Vasios, Martin Leeds, Mark Taylor, and Jonathan Adler. I am also indebted to my colleagues at Manhattan College for tolerating a sport historian in their ranks, especially Frederick Schweitzer, Julie Leininger Pycior, Claire Nolte, Joseph Castora, Juliana Gilheany, and Jeff Horn.

I also appreciate the help provided to me by the staffs of the Cardinal Hayes Library at Manhattan College, the New York Public Library, the Historical Society of Pennsylvania, the Free Library of Philadelphia, the Western Reserve Historical Society, the National Baseball Hall of Fame and Museum, and the Seeley G. Mudd Manuscript Library at Princeton University.

I am grateful to all of the editorial staff at Princeton University Press who assisted with the publication of this book, and especially to Thomas LeBien. He was consistently encouraging and enthusiastic about this project, and his criticisms and suggestions were always insightful and helpful. I also thank the University of Illinois Press for permission to include excerpts from my book, *The Creation of American Team Sports: Baseball and Cricket, 1838–72* (Champaign, IL, 1989).

To my wife of more than three decades, Susan Lavitt Kirsch, I offer my love and my lifetime of devotion for caring for me during all of my life's trials. Her gifts to me have been priceless, and I am truly sorry that I have not been able to pay back all of the debts that I owe to her.

I dedicate this book to my only child, Adam Lavitt Kirsch. He did not inherit the Kirsch family baseball gene, but he did give me much greater gifts beyond the world of sports. I honor him for his brilliant mind, his strength of character, and his lively personality. He is simply the best son a father could ever have.

Baseball in Blue and Gray

The Rise of Baseball

I n Albert G. Spalding's classic early history and celebration of baseball, *America's National Game,* he included a long newspaper description of the game as it was played by country boys long before the time of Doubleday or the Knickerbockers. The author of the story, undated from the *Memphis Appeal,* recalled that on Saturday afternoons "the neighborhood boys met on some cropped pasture, and whether ten or forty, every one was to take part in the game." He explained that "self-appointed leaders chose sides and whirled a bat that decided who would hit first. The bat was "a stout paddle, with a blade two inches thick and four inches wide." The ball "was usually made on the spot by some boy offering up his woolen socks as an oblation, and these were raveled and wound around a bullet, a handful of strips cut from a rubber overshoe, a piece of cork or almost anything." The field might have four, six, or seven bases, which "were not equidistant, but were marked by any fortuitous rock, or shrub, or depression in the ground where the steers were wont to bellow and paw up the earth." Home plate was "the den." In addition, "there were no masks, or mitts, or protectors. There was no science or chicanery, now called 'headwork.' " The pitcher's object "was to throw a ball that could be hit. The paddleman's object was to hit the ball, and if he struck at it— which he need not do unless he chose—and missed it, the catcher, standing well back, tried to catch it" for an out. After hitting the ball the batsman ran from base to base. "There was no effort to pounce upon a base runner and touch him with the ball. Anyone having the ball could throw it at him, and if it hit him he was 'dead'—almost literally sometimes. If he dodged the ball, he kept on running till the den was reached. . . . No matter how many players were on a side, each and every one had to be put out." There was no umpire, and "very little wrangling." The score was kept by someone cutting notches in a stick, and "the runs in an afternoon ran into the hundreds."

Before the Civil War there were numerous variations on the rules and customs reported in this reminiscence. Young men in Philadelphia, Boston, and New York City adapted and tried to improve the ball games that city youth and rural boys had enjoyed for generations. In 1831 a few young sportsmen began a new era of Philadelphia ball playing when they crossed the Delaware River for regular contests of "two old cat" at Camden, New Jersey. Before long they had recruited enough players for Saturday afternoon townball, despite being "frequently reproved and censured by their friends for degrading themselves by indulging in such childish amusement." These ball players competed on public grounds, where neither rent nor permission was required, and made their own bats and balls. After another group of townball enthusiasts joined them in 1833, the two formally merged and organized the Olympic Ball Club, drawing up a constitution and field rules to govern their play.

These pioneer athletes were principally merchants and "respectable and well-known citizens of Philadelphia," several of whom later distinguished themselves in their city's business and professional life. They were remembered as a "conservative and temperate body of gentlemen who enjoyed mixing their sports with good conversation, wit, food, and drink." A highlight of each season was the Fourth of July celebration, when their president read the Declaration of Independence and the members sang songs and heard "an address delivered for the perpetuation of the Stars and Stripes." Thus townball displayed an early association between ball play and nationalism that would increase significantly during the Civil War era and well beyond into the twentieth century. That pastime remained popular in the Philadelphia area through the late 1850s, with several

2

clubs in Camden and Germantown joining Philadelphia's Olympics, Excelsiors, and Athletics. There is some evidence that emigrants from the City of Brotherly Love carried their sport to Cincinnati, Ohio, and neighboring towns in northern Kentucky, where townball flourished before the Civil War.

Townball players in the Philadelphia region generally made their own bats and balls and competed according to rules that resembled English rounders. Brief newspaper accounts and box scores suggest that they played with eleven men on a side for either two or eleven innings. All men batted in an inning when only two innings were played. When one out retired a side the game lasted eleven or more innings. They also seemed to have used stakes as bases. Detailed box scores gave the total score, including runs per inning. Typically the victorious team scored at least 75 runs. The box scores also listed statistics for each man for "Fielding" and "How Put Out." The "Fielding" section listed numbers for balls caught on the "fly," on the first "bound," and "behind" (probably tipped balls received by the catcher). The "How Put Out" part listed "fly," "bound," "behind," and also "no balls" and "On Stakes." "No balls" probably counted strikeouts (three missed swings). "On Stakes" likely meant runners put out on the bases, although there is no indication if runners were tagged out or if they were hit with balls thrown at them by fielders.

Yankee varieties of townball were called "base" or "roundball." In 1856 a Boston enthusiast described that sport as "truly national," a game that "is played by the school boys in every country village in New England, as well as in the parks of many of our New England cities." He continued: "Base used to be a favorite game with the students of the English High and Latin Schools of Boston, a few years ago. . . . Base is also a favorite game upon the green in front of village school-houses in the country throughout New England; and in this city, on Fast Day . . . Boston Common is covered with amateur parties of men and boys playing Base." Boston's truckmen attracted large crowds of spectators, who admired their "supply of muscle that renders them able to outdo all competitors in striking and throwing."

3

This "Massachusetts game" generally matched sides of eight to fifteen men on a square field with bases or tall stakes (up to five feet high) at each corner. The batter stood midway between first and fourth (home) base and tried to hit a ball "made of yarn, tightly wound round a lump or cork or India rubber, and covered with smooth calf-skin in quarters. . . the seams closed snugly, and not raised, lest they should blister the hands of the thrower and catcher." The round bat varied from three to three and a half feet in length and was often "a portion of stout rake or pitchfork handle . . . wielded generally in one hand by the muscular young players at the country schools." The pitcher threw the ball swiftly overhand (not under-hand, as in the New York version), "with a vigor . . . that made it whistle through the air, and stop with a solid *smack* in the catcher's hands." The receiver had to be able "to catch expertly a swiftly deliv-ered ball, or he would be admonished of his inexpertness by a request from some player to 'butter his fingers'!" The batter could strike the ball in any direction, there being no foul territory. James D'Wolf Lovett recalled that when he played as a boy for a junior club near Boston, batters sometimes shortened up on the bat, grasping it near the middle, "and by a quick turn of the wrist [struck] the ball, as it passed them, in the same direction in which it was thrown, thus avoiding the fielders and giving the striker a good start on the bases." After hitting the ball, the striker ran around the bases until he was put out or remained safely on a base. He could be retired if the catcher caught three missed balls, or if a hit ball was caught on the fly, or if he was struck by a thrown ball while running the bases (called "soak-ing" or "burning" a runner). Usually one out ended the inning, and the first team to score a fixed number of runs won the game.

The first modern baseball organization in Massachusetts was the Olympic Club of Boston, whose members began playing in 1854, formally established the club in 1856, and published rules and regu-lations in 1857. That year brought many spirited intrasquad games and matches against newly formed clubs on Boston Common. In late June about 2,000 spectators attended the first round of an informal Massachusetts championship tournament between the Olympics and the Wassapoag Ball Club of Sharon. Each team had twelve men to a side, twenty-five runs were needed to win the game, and three victories decided the match. Wassapoag defeated the Olympics but then lost to the Unions of Medway. A dispute over rules canceled the return contest for the title and eventually led to the Massachusetts Baseball Convention in Dedham in May 1858, at which the Massachusetts Association of Base Ball Players was created and a constitution, bylaws, and rules and regulations were approved.

At this convention representatives of the Tri-Mountain club tried to persuade the delegates to adopt the code of the New York version of the game, which had been created by the New York Knickerbocker club back in the 1840s. It featured a diamond instead of a square for the bases, with the batter standing at home plate. The New York regulations also stipulated that the ball had to be pitched underhand, not thrown overhand; that a ball knocked outside the range of first or third base was foul; and that a player was out if a hit ball was caught on the fly or first bounce, or if a fielder held the ball on a base before the runner arrived, or if, between bases, a fielder touched the runner with the ball. "Soaking" the runner was prohibited, three outs retired the side, and twenty-one runs (called aces) decided the game, provided each side had an equal number of outs. But the majority of the Massachusetts men preferred their traditional style of play and rejected the upstart New York version. They approved rules which formally established a game similar to traditional New England townball, with a square field, overhand pitching, no foul territory, ten to twelve men per side, one out to retire all, and victory belonging to the team that first scored one hundred runs.

The convention's labors bore fruit, for during the years remaining before the Civil War the "Massachusetts Game" flourished. In September 1858 a Boston correspondent to the *New York Clipper* reported a sharp increase in public interest in both cricket and baseball, which he attributed in part to the favorable notices from the local press and to the cooperation of city merchants who closed their doors on summer Saturday afternoons. He also credited much of the excitement to the recent formation of the state association of baseball players, adding: "Base Ball is getting to be the most predominant institution of this State. Clubs are now forming in every country town and village, and a great many matches have been played this season." Proof of the baseball fever sweeping New England was evident in a September 1859 match played for the Massachusetts state championship between the Unions of Medway and the Winthrops of Holliston. Several railroads issued excursion tickets to Boston's Agricultural Fair Grounds, where a large crowd bet heavily on the two-day encounter, won by the Unions, 100–71.

While the Massachusetts form of baseball thrived during the 1850s, it faced a formidable rival in the New York City version, which mushroomed in popularity during these years. Modern baseball derives most immediately from the New York version, created by the Knickerbockers during the mid-1840s. As Melvin Adelman has shown, the majority of these sportsmen were prosperous (but not affluent) middle-class merchants, bankers, doctors, lawyers, clerks, and other white-collar workers. None belonged to the city's elite, although a few ranked just one rung below the city's aristocracy. These first ball players sought health, exercise, and good fellowship in their sport and were not very much interested in seeking out other nines for interclub competition. Perhaps because of their defensiveness about playing a child's game, or because they valued privacy, they did not seek publicity in New York's daily or weekly papers.

One of the chief organizers of the Knickerbockers in 1845 was Alexander J. Cartwright, Jr. While he certainly deserves far more recognition than Doubleday for the creation of baseball, it is doubtful whether his contribution was so critical as to justify his later enshrinement in the Hall of Fame. The son of a shipping proprietor, Cartwright began his business career as a clerk and then joined with his brother to open a bookstore and stationery shop during the mid-1840s. He belonged to a volunteer fire company and played baseball with friends and fellow firefighters on the east side of Manhattan. Some baseball historians believe that Cartwright was the one who first suggested that the Knickerbockers try a diamond instead of a square for the bases, with the batter standing at home plate. He is often credited with the codification of its first rules, but it is more likely that he shared that task with several of his teammates—

6

especially William R. Wheaton and William H. Tucker. As described above, the distinctive features of their regulations included the infield diamond for bases, underhand pitching, foul territory, the force out and tag play for retiring runners, three outs to a side, and victory to the first team to score twenty-one runs.

The Knickerbockers played intrasquad games in the Murray Hill section of Manhattan, then in 1846 moved to the Elysian Fields of Hoboken, New Jersey. There they competed in a few matches against other teams, including a semi-organized outfit called the New York Club. The Gothams (originally named the Washingtons), the next formal baseball club, began play in the early 1850s at the St. George Cricket Club ground in Harlem. The Eagles (1852) and the Empires (1854), both of New York City, and the Excelsiors (1854) of South Brooklyn increased to five the number of teams playing by the Knickerbocker rules before 1855. During the next six years a veritable baseball mania overtook the greater New York City region, as more than two hundred junior and senior clubs sprang into action in Brooklyn, Queens, Manhattan, Westchester, and northern New Jersey.

Neither Abner Doubleday or Alexander Cartwright or any other person created the modern sport of baseball; rather, it evolved in stages from earlier bat and ball games. Historians today believe that Henry Chadwick was correct in linking baseball to English rounders. Robert Henderson, for example, has shown that early nineteenth-century American sports books printed rules for rounders under the heading "Base, or Goal Ball." Townball seems to have been an Americanized variation of rounders, and both probably developed as team versions of the traditional game of "old cat." Strictly speaking, modern baseball is a refined, United States variety of townball and therefore is certainly an indigenous sport. While its ancestry is English, its essence is clearly American. Chadwick made this point as early as 1860 when he wrote that, although baseball was "of English origin, it has been so modified and improved of late years in this country, as almost to deprive it of any of its original features beyond the mere groundwork of the game." In 1864 *Wilkes' Spirit of the Times* compared the children's pastime of rounders with

7

1. Henry Chadwick (1824–1908). Known as the "father of baseball," he was an English immigrant who became a sporting journalist, promoter of the early game, and inventor of the first system for compiling box scores and statistics. In the early twentieth century he argued that baseball derived from rounders, an old English pastime. Used with permission of the National Baseball Hall of Fame Library, Cooperstown, NY.

the adult sport of baseball, describing the former as "a very simple game, and designed only for recreation during the intervals from study in schools, and . . . entirely devoid of the manly features that characterize base-ball as played in this country."

Despite their different views on the linkage of rounders and baseball, Spalding, Chadwick, and sporting journalists agreed that a distinctly American process of modernization changed a traditional folk game into a late nineteenth-century sport. This transformation began in Philadelphia, Boston, and New York City during the period 1830–60, as each of these cities developed versions of baseball. During the 1850s these types competed for dominance with each other and also with the English game of cricket—the first modern team sport in the United States. By the Civil War the New York City variety had established itself in most parts of the nation, and by the mid-1860s it had defeated its rivals to become the favored form of ball play in the United States.

Before 1861, then, the three leading centers of adult organized ball playing in America were Philadelphia, Boston, and New York. Prior to the outbreak of war the "New York game" was rapidly invading New England, the Philadelphia area, and even southern and western states in a drive to become the nation's most popular team sport. How exactly did the New York version of the game spread? Why did it surpass competing versions of ball playing? And why did it prevail over cricket, which was firmly established in many American cities and towns before baseball burst upon the sporting scene?

During the late 1850s New York City baseball enthusiasts taught the rules of their game to friends in neighboring towns and distant cities. Edward G. Saltzman, a member of the New York Gothams, helped to found Boston's Tri-Mountain Base Ball Club in 1857. He became president of the new organization and taught the members the New York rules, which were new to Boston and which the club adopted. Also, the treasurer of the Tri-Mountains, while visiting New York, watched the Empires practice and was invited to play with the Gothams. Personal contact and visits helped to plant the "New York game" in Baltimore as well. In 1858 Joseph Leggett of the famous Brooklyn Excelsiors invited George Beam, a wholesale grocer in Baltimore, to see a game in New York. Beam became a baseball enthusiast and organized a ball club (also named the Excelsiors) in his home city, made up primarily of businessmen. Within a year there were several other nines in Baltimore.

Long-distance geographical mobility brought New York baseball to the Midwest and the West Coast. Theodore Frost (from Rochester College) and Mathew M. Yorston introduced baseball to Cincinnati in 1860, recruiting high school students and businessmen to form the Live Oak Base Ball Club. They worked hard to demonstrate the superiority of this new game over townball, and before long the city's Excelsior and Buckeye townball clubs adopted the rules of the "New York game." Alexander Cartwright crossed the Great Plains in the 1840s, apparently teaching the game he helped to invent to interested sportsmen. Though he stayed only briefly in northern California before moving on to Hawaii, the first California club was organized in San Francisco in 1858; two years later, M.E. Gelston of the New York Eagles, an all-star player in the 1858 New York versus Brooklyn series, became captain of a San Francisco nine, which renamed itself the Eagle club in his honor. At a November 1860 tournament Gelston's team defeated a Sacramento club, captained by E. N. Robinson, formerly of the Putnams of Brooklyn. Thus an old New York—Brooklyn rivalry was re-enacted on the Pacific Coast, perhaps a foreboding of the more famous migrations of entire New York and Brooklyn clubs nearly one hundred years later. Gelston and Robinson were followed by many other easterners who took the sport along on their journeys to the Golden State. William and James Shepard, two New Yorkers who had played with famous ball stars of the 1850s, traversed the plains on their way to San Francisco in 1861, where they continued to enjoy the game they had learned in the East.

Intercity competition was another means of popularizing the "New York game" before the Civil War. While baseball nines were not as mobile as cricket elevens during this era, there were a few urban rivalries that gave the new sport a big boost. Perhaps none was more intense than that between New York and Brooklyn clubs. Since civic pride was keen on both sides of the East River, it was only natural for the leading Brooklyn teams to challenge their New York City counterparts to a three-game series between their best players. In 1858 *Porter's Spirit*, in a burst of hyperbole, predicted that a crowd of one hundred thousand would see "one of the grandest tournaments that has ever been witnessed in the history of the world." Although Brooklyn lost the 1858 series, the following year its baseball fraternity established its dominance over neighboring teams. That city surpassed all its rivals in both the number of clubs and the quality of their performance. As the *Brooklyn Eagle* crowed, "Nowhere has the National game of Baseball taken firmer hold than in Brooklyn and nowhere are there better players." That paper noted every triumph over a New York club, at one point proclaiming: "If we are ahead of the big city in nothing else, we can beat her in baseball." With the Manhattan-Brooklyn competition as a model, Newark, Bloomfield, Jersey City, New Brunswick, and other New Jersey towns inaugurated spirited intercity baseball competitions. Teams from Baltimore and Washington, D.C., followed suit in 1860. Whenever baseball fever infected a new city, it was only a short time before its best teams looked elsewhere for other nines to conquer.

Outside the greater New York metropolitan area the 1860 tours of the Brooklyn Excelsiors excited thousands of sportsmen throughout upstate New York, Baltimore, and Philadelphia. In July this "crack club" visited Albany, Troy, Buffalo, Rochester, and Newburgh, and news of its victories flashed across the state's telegraph wires. Spalding believed that these exhibitions inspired young men to hope "that they might win for their cities a glory akin to that which had been achieved for [Brooklyn]." According to the *Clipper*, the Excelsiors's visit advanced baseball in Baltimore by three or four years, and the paper predicted that their excursion would stir up interest in the sport in other cities further south. The Excelsiors concluded their travels in Philadelphia, where they defeated a select nine from the local clubs that had adopted the New York rules that season.

11

Partly because of this visit, baseball in Philadelphia exploded in popularity. The New York version of the sport soon conquered the City of Brotherly Love, leaving townball a quaint relic of the past.

Championship match competition among the leading clubs also gave the New York game a huge boost prior to the Civil War. The Brooklyn teams monopolized public interest before 1861 as early fans followed the exploits of that city's Excelsiors, Atlantics, and Eckfords. The rivalries among these nines also carried social class overtones, since the membership of the Excelsiors included many merchants, lawyers, doctors, and other professionals, while the men of the Atlantics and Eckfords were skilled workers. The Atlantics, founded in 1855 and named after a Brooklyn street, enrolled many butchers and others from the food preparation trades. The Eckfords were mostly shipwrights and mechanics. Their seven founders named their association after Henry Eckford, a Scottish immigrant who became a prominent Brooklyn shipbuilder.

During the late summer of 1860 a three game championship series between the Excelsiors and the Atlantics became both a showcase for baseball's early success and also an ominous foreboding of future troubles. A riotous scene at the third and deciding game resulted in much ill will. These two crack teams had split the opening contests—the Excelsiors won the first game easily but lost the second by a single run. On August 23 they met on the neutral site of the Putnam Base Ball Club's grounds in Brooklyn in front of a crowd estimated at about 15,000 fans. The excitement among the baseball fraternity was intense, as rumors circulated that the Excelsiors would not be allowed to win a close contest. During the early play one of the Atlantics agitated part of the crowd by refusing to yield immediately to an umpire's call. Then, in the top of the sixth inning, with the Excelsiors ahead 8–6, a group of rowdies renewed their "insulting epithets and loud comments on the decision of the umpire." Joseph Leggett, the Excelsiors's captain, warned the spectators that his team would withdraw if the hooting continued. Members of the Atlantics appealed to their supporters to let the game go on, as one hundred policemen tried to restrain the unruly crowd. But the troublemakers only increased their yelling and abuse of the umpire and the Excelsiors, prompting Leggett to order his players off the field. A large mob pursued them and pelted their omnibus with stones as they drove off. Most newspapers blamed the disorders and interference on gambling and condemned the behavior of those spectators who had disrupted the contest. It was unfortunate that "sports which are healthful and respectable in themselves should be rendered disreputable by their surroundings," commented the *Brooklyn Daily Eagle*, which then added that "a little further decadence will reduce the attendance at ball matches to the level of the prize ring and the race course."

Baseball also benefited greatly from the publicity provided by the New York City weekly sporting periodicals. The *Clipper*, *Porter's Spirit*, and *Wilkes' Spirit* published editorials extolling the game and printed all the convention news as well as detailed stories and box scores on major and minor matches. While these periodicals also printed material on townball and the "Massachusetts game," the New York City version got far more space. Before the Civil War even local daily newspapers began irregular coverage of baseball, giving the sport a crucial boost in numerous cities and towns across America.

Among all of the early sportswriters, none was a more tireless advocate of baseball than Henry Chadwick. Born in Exeter, England in 1824, he moved to America with his family in 1837. He inherited both a love of journalism and a passion for outdoor recreation from his father, an editor. As a young man Chadwick was a good athlete who became a skilled cricketer but initially had little enthusiasm for townball, partly because he disliked being hit in the ribs with accurately thrown balls. In 1868 he recalled that his passion for baseball began in 1856 when he watched an exciting match at Hoboken's Elysian Fields between the Eagle and Gotham teams. As an active member of the New York Cricket Club and Manhattan's National Base Ball Club during the 1850s he played and reported on both games during their infancy in the United States. A life-long resident of Brooklyn, he wrote first for the *Clipper* and later for the *Brooklyn Eagle*, the *New York Times*, the *Herald*, the *World*, the *Sun*, and the *Tribune*. Through countless articles and his editing of *Beadles's Dime Base Ball Player* and later the *Spalding Baseball Guides* he exerted a powerful influence on the development of baseball rules. Perhaps even more importantly, he devised scoring systems that helped reporters compile box scores, averages, and other statistics. Through this contribution he provided an invaluable means of communicating the action on the field to innumerable fans across the nation. Always a Victorian gentleman, he stressed the health, moral, and character-building advantages of the sport, repeatedly condemning rowdyism and gambling whenever they threatened to ruin baseball's reputation.

Individuals, clubs, and the press all gave baseball a big boost during the 1850s, but perhaps the key event in the sport's early modernization was the founding of its first centralized governing body—the National Association of Base Ball Players, or the NABBP. As historian Harold Seymour has pointed out, the creation of this organization in 1857 was crucial in baseball's history, launching an era in which players met annually to refine the rules, resolve disputes, and control the sport's development. When the 1858 convention decided to perpetuate itself by drawing up a permanent constitution, bylaws, and rules of the game, self-designation as a *national* association indicated ambitious designs. Although only clubs from the New York City vicinity were represented, the aim was to rule the continent. Its hubris did not go unnoticed. The *Clipper* scolded the leadership by pointing out that "the convention seems to be rather sectional and selfish in its proceedings... there having been no invitations sent to clubs in other States." Furthermore, the association was "a mere local organization, bearing no *State* existence even—to say nothing of a *National* one." The paper urged delegates to invite baseball players from everywhere "to compete with them, and endeavor to make the game what it should be—a truly National one." The last two meetings of the NABBP before the Civil War did attract representatives from Boston, New Haven, Baltimore, Washington, D.C., and Detroit. Most encouraging was the attendance of five Philadelphia clubs in December 1860, which reflected that city's recent baseball mania. Thus while the NABBP was still dominated by New York and Brooklyn clubs, in just a few years it had considerably broadened its base and its influence, prompting the *Clipper* to state in 1860 that "this association is national in every respect, and is intended to include delegates from every club in the Union."

In the long run, the most important work of the national conventions involved rule revisions. The 1857 meeting adopted virtually all of the Knickerbocker regulations but changed the method of deciding the outcome of matches, switching from awarding victory to the first team to score twenty-one runs to awarding it to that team which scored the highest number after nine full innings. One year later the delegates approved a rule that permitted the umpire to call a strike if a batter repeatedly refused to swing at "good balls." The most heated debate occurred over the rule that counted a batter out if a fielder caught the ball on the first bounce. Opponents of this rule wished to replace it with the "fly game" rule, which preserved all of the other modes of retiring a runner but mandated that a ball caught on the first bound was fair and in play. They argued that the bound rule made baseball less scientific and "manly." For a time, tradition and conservatism prevailed as delegates repeatedly voted down the fly rule. That innovation finally passed in 1864, however, in the very different circumstances that prevailed during the Civil War.

One of the stated objectives of the NABBP was "the cultivation of kindly feelings among the different members of Base-Ball clubs." To promote good sportsmanship and friendly competition, the association passed several regulations concerning the eligibility of players for club matches. In particular, it required competitors to be regular members of the clubs they represented for at least thirty days prior to a contest, the purpose being to prohibit any club's use of talented outsiders to gain an advantage. The 1859 gathering prohibited gambling by contestants and umpires, as well as interference by spectators. It also barred professionals by prohibiting any player who received compensation from competing in a match. The banning of paid players was clearly an attempt to preserve baseball as a recreation rather than as a vocation, yet it was not universally popular within the game's fraternity. The *Clipper* questioned whether outlawing professionals had "something of an aristocratic odor" and, as such, exhibited "a rather uncharitable disposition toward poor players." But Francis Pidgeon, a skilled craftsman and member of Brooklyn's Eckford club, did not want to see the more affluent clubs hire the most skilled athletes. He maintained that the rule was passed "to protect ourselves against the influence of money, and give 'honest poverty' a fair chance, and in a struggle for supremacy between clubs to let skill, courage, and endurance decide who shall be the victors." Undoubtedly gentlemen's clubs (such as the Knickerbockers) abhorred the idea of playing for money; and men like Pidgeon realized that while professionalism might aid some indigent players, it would hurt many artisan nines.

The creation of baseball coincided with an intense wave of political and cultural nationalism that swept the country during the middle decades of the nineteenth century. In the domestic arena, the rise of sectionalism in the South threatened the unity of the nation and also made northerners and westerners more conscious of their attachment to the Union. The influx of foreigners inflamed patriotic passions, as many citizens resented the arrival of thousands of Irish, Germans, English, and other Europeans. In foreign affairs the United States defeated Mexico in a war that secured Texas and brought Utah, New Mexico, and California under the Stars and Stripes. A negotiated settlement with Great Britain over the Oregon boundary averted another war, although Anglo-American relations remained tense. As "Young America" became a popular slogan of the Democratic Party, the United States expanded its trade and influence into Latin America and Asia. In their cultural lives, Americans strove for a literary and artistic independence from European (and especially British) influence that would match their political separation from the Old World. Cultural nationalism also appeared in the realm of sport, as Brother Jonathan challenged John Bull in horse racing, yachting, and boxing.

Given this atmosphere of chauvinism, it is understandable why the idea of a national game appealed to the American imagination during this era. But in the 1850s it was not yet clear which sport would earn that distinction. In addition to the multiple forms of baseball, cricket was well established in many cities, especially Philadelphia, and initially enjoyed more extensive newspaper coverage in the New York City sporting press. But although the English game of cricket was America's first modern team sport, by 1860 it was already clear that baseball had surpassed it to earn recognition as the country's national pastime. Cricket was attractive to thousands of sportsmen, but it suffered from serious disadvantages in its competition with baseball. It required more care for its grounds and was more expensive to play. Its association with the British alienated some, especially as Englishmen generally used the game to reaffirm their ethnic heritage. Cricket's subtleties and skill requirements were also quite challenging to the uninitiated. Spectators who were unfamiliar with the sport disliked the length of the matches and their slow pace and lack of action. Americans who tried to adapt the game to their own sporting tastes discovered that its English adherents preferred to retain old customs. The tide of modernization carried baseball players along in a surge of time-consciousness, and they came to prize action and speed; but cricketers resisted this momentum.

References to the "national game of baseball" appeared frequently in the daily and sporting press throughout the late 1850s, even before the modern form actually achieved a truly national scope. Commenting on the work of the first baseball convention in January 1857, *Porter's Spirit* urged that baseball "ought to be looked upon in this country with the same national enthusiasm as Cricket and Football are regarded in the British Islands. . . . We recommend it because there should be some one game peculiar to the citizens of the United States. The Germans have brought hither their Turnverein Association. . . . and it certainly was quite time that some attempt was made to set up a game that could be termed a 'Native American Sport.' " In 1860 the *Clipper* confirmed that baseball "may now be considered the National game of ball."

The early association between baseball and American nationalism appears in several symbols that players adopted for their clubs, including names and flags. Many selected such patriotic titles as Young America, Columbia, Union, Independent, Eagle, American, Continental, Empire, National, Liberty, and Pioneer. Others honored such heroes as George Washington, Alexander Hamilton, James Madison, Thomas Jefferson, Andrew Jackson, and Benjamin Franklin. Flag presentations by women to members of athletic clubs or military regiments were common both in Europe and the United States during the nineteenth century. The American flag was also commonly used to consecrate baseball. For example, in 1859 in the small town of Danvers Centre, Massachusetts, a bevy of ladies presented the Stars and Stripes to the local Essex Base Ball Club. Their delegates praised the men for their healthy recreation, which the ladies thought was far preferable to the frequenting of "the gilded saloon, or the table of chance." When Amherst College defeated Williams College in the first intercollegiate baseball match in 1859, some spectators on the nearby roof of the Young Ladies Institute waved a "Star Spangled Banner" at the players. In 1860 a song sheet cover for the "Live Oak Polka," dedicated to the Live Oak Base Ball Club of Rochester, New York, featured both a shield adorned with stars and stripes and a draped American flag. Baseball had clearly begun to acquire familiar connections with love of country, freedom, virtue, morality, the work ethic, and other traditional American values.

Another indication of the connection between baseball and nationalism appeared in the presidential campaign of 1860. Abraham Lincoln's rise to political prominence, his election as the nation's chief executive, and his term as commander-in-chief occurred during the years when the game was achieving increasing popularity in all regions. The earliest association between Lincoln and baseball appeared in a Currier & Ives political cartoon published in November 1860, shortly after Lincoln defeated three rivals to claim the presidency. The print was entitled: "THE NATIONAL GAME. THREE 'OUTS' AND ONE 'RUN', Abraham Winning the Ball." It depicted all four candidates holding baseball bats inscribed with their respective political positions—"fusion" for John Bell of the border state Constitutional Union party; "non-intervention" (on

2. "The Live Oak Polka." This 1860 song sheet cover includes a dedication to the Live Oak Base Ball Club of Rochester, N.Y. Note the American shield, flag, and bunting. The diamond shaped field indicates that the Live Oaks followed the New York rules. Used with permission of the National Baseball Hall of Fame Library, Cooperstown, NY.

the slavery issue) for Stephen Douglas, a northern Democrat; and "slavery extension" for John C. Breckinridge, a southern Democrat. Lincoln's bat is labeled "equal rights and free territory," and he is also raising a ball, signifying that he was the winner. The words in each figure's text bubble contain the baseball slang of the era: Bell thinks that it is "very singular that we three should strike 'foul' and be 'put out' while old Abe made such a 'good lick.'" Douglas explains: "That's because he had that confounded rail, to strike with.

19

I thought our fusion would be a 'short stop' to his career." Breckin-ridge, holding his nose and turning away, proclaims: "I guess I'd bet-ter leave for Kentucky, for I smell something strong around here, and begin to think that we are completely 'skunk'd.' " The victorious Lincoln has the last word: "Gentlemen, if any of you should ever take a hand in another match at this game, remember that you must have 'a good bat' and strike a 'fair ball' to make a 'clean score' & a 'home run.' " Clearly, Currier & Ives believed that its customers would easily relate the sport and its special language to the presiden-tial campaign of that season.

A geography of baseball before 1861 illustrates the growing national popularity of the game. Most formally organized teams were located in cities, but a few also appeared in rural areas. Among the competing versions, the NABBP rules were well known, dominating in most of the larger communities. The hotbeds of baseball fever were in the New York City vicinity, the Hudson River Valley, central and upstate New York, and the Boston area; and during the 1850s the game also took root in numerous eastern, western, and southern localities.

In the northeast the "Massachusetts Game" remained the sportsmen's favorite form of ball play in New England, even as the NABBP rules made inroads. Although some thought that the Mas-sachusetts version was more "scientific," it was obvious that the NABBP/New York style of play was winning converts. A report from the Bay State noted that fifty-nine clubs observed the Massachusetts rules while eighteen followed those of New York. In the New York City vicinity the NABBP rules naturally dominated, with only a few pockets of old-style townball remaining. Manhattan had dozens of clubs competing there and across the river in Hoboken, New Jersey. But the real center of baseball mania was Brooklyn, which fielded over one hundred junior and senior clubs before 1861. Over in New Jersey, at least 130 baseball clubs were active between 1855 and 1860, with Newark alone accounting for 36 junior and senior orga-nizations and Jersey City adding another 42. The first club in Phila-delphia to play the New York style of baseball was the Penn Tigers

THE NATIONAL GAME. THREE "OUTS" AND ONE "RUN".
ABRAHAM WINNING THE BALL.

3. "The National Game. Three 'Outs' And One 'Run.'" This Currier and Ives political cartoon features the four presidential candidates in the election of 1860. The title and the association of baseball with that campaign represent an early identification of the sport as the national pastime. Library of Congress, Prints and Photographs Division.

(later the Winonas), during an intrasquad match in late 1858. The next year brought Philadelphia's first full season of interclub play, as about a dozen nines laid out diamonds and played a primitive form of baseball. The "New York game" took a major step toward conquering the City of Brotherly Love in 1860, when the Olympic Ball Club dropped townball after nearly thirty years and adopted the NABBP rules of play. Townball and the "Massachusetts game" still lingered in Pittsburgh and in such rural hamlets as Allegheny, Mauch Chunk, and Conneaut Lake.

The Midwest and West also shared in the excitement over baseball. Baseball in general and the New York version in particular were becoming familiar pastimes across the continent prior to the Civil War. Larger midwest cities such as Chicago, Cleveland, Detroit, Milwaukee, and St. Paul and smaller towns such as Nininger City, Minnesota territory, Oberlin, Ohio, Davenport, Iowa, Fox Lake, Wisconsin, all reported clubs and matches to the New York sporting journals. On the Pacific Coast, California claimed at least five teams in San Francisco, Stockton, and Sacramento, and several tournaments played according to the NABBP regulations in the fall of 1860 created much interest in the new team sport in the Golden State. A baseball fanatic from Boston, Brooklyn, or Philadelphia had a pretty good chance of finding a ball game as he traveled westward before 1861.

As the "New York game" swept the ball-playing fraternities in many antebellum cities and towns, it also penetrated into more remote areas. When its advocates introduced the sport into small communities, they repeated familiar patterns of cultural interaction between rural and urban America. Folk versions of baseball originated in country villages, but the modern sport was rationalized and modernized in the emerging commercial and industrial cities of the mid-nineteenth century. Then it was re-exported into the hinterland, where it prospered. The *New York Times* captured this process in action in an 1858 editorial: "We predict that [baseball] will spread from the city to the country, and revive there, where it was dying out, a love of the noble game." There are many instances of city players instructing farm boys in the latest "scientific" rules and techniques of the sport. For example, in November 1860 several members of the Athletics of Philadelphia journeyed to Mauch Chunk to play ball with some of that Pennsylvania town's young men. The Athletics and their hosts agreed to one contest of townball and one of New York–style baseball, thus introducing the more modern game into a rural area. In 1866 an early surveyor of American sport cred-

4. "Home Run Quick Step." This song sheet cover, published around 1860, includes a dedication to the members of the Mercantile Base Ball Club of Philadelphia, PA. The Mercantiles were among the first Philadelphia players to adopt the New York game. Used with permission of the Historical Society of Pennsylvania, Philadelphia, PA. Thomas S. Sinclair, lithographer, Bb07B291.

ited the Athletics with having "done more to advance the popularity of the game, by visits to towns and villages where baseball was previously unknown, than almost any other club in the United States." While the teaching of modern baseball proceeded, the sport never lost its special quality of being part pastoral country game and part scientific, rational urban amusement.

Modern forms of baseball encountered more resistance in the South than in other parts of the nation. But even there, while slave masters on plantations and leading citizens in inland towns showed little interest in the game, prominent merchants and other citizens of a few southern seaports adopted it with enthusiasm. Historian Kenneth Greenberg has argued that southern masters were indifferent to baseball because the sport "seemed to embody a set of values at odds with their culture." According to his view, men of honor disliked such elements of the game as the act of running after a batter hit the ball, because of the role reversal and change of status as a hitter ceased being a subject and became an object pursued by the fielders. Although Greenberg cites just one example of a planter refusing to run after a hit and cursing the game after he was tagged out, it is probably true that most masters had some difficulty with the democratic elements of the new sport. Baseball had no clear fixed or privileged positions, not even the pitcher, who was supposed to throw "good balls" that players could strike.

While southern plantation owners showed little enthusiasm for baseball, there is some evidence that their slaves occasionally enjoyed some forms of ball games. Historian Kenneth Wiggins has compiled a few cases of slaves who recalled playing games that resembled rounders or townball before and just after the Civil War. For example, while James Henry Stith of Arkansas was born after slavery ended, as a young child he remembered seeing older boys playing baseball, and he speculated that they must have learned it "in slave time." Another Southerner, Henry Baker, remembered participating in townball on a plantation in Alabama after the war.

A good example of both a sports journalist's propaganda in behalf of baseball and the lack of enthusiasm for the sport in a major southern town is Henry Chadwick's personal campaign to stimulate interest in the game in Richmond, Virginia. In 1848 Chadwick married a young lady from that city, and he and his wife regularly visited her relatives there. While in town he tried to organize both cricket and baseball clubs, with little success. In March 1861 the *Clipper* expressed surprise at the tardy development of these sports in a town with good fields and plenty of young men with ample leisure time, noting that "as organizations already so successfully commenced in Baltimore and Washington have initiated the institution in Southern cities, we hope Richmond will this season follow suit, by getting up a club of her own." The paper advised any interested parties to contact "H.C." in the hope that a nine might be formed by mid-April. A few weeks later, however, the firing on Fort Sumter and the ensuing Civil War spoiled plans to initiate baseball in a city that soon became the capital of the Confederacy.

Yet several southern seaports and a few river communities were more hospitable to baseball, in part because of the model and tutelage provided by touring ball players and visiting businessmen from the North. Although southern urbanization lagged behind that of the North during the antebellum era, the South's larger cities did exhibit certain cultural characteristics similar to their northern counterparts, including baseball. In fact, the sport that was conquering northeast communities made its first inroads in southern towns. Early baseball was an urban phenomenon, better suited to the values and needs of merchants, clerks, journalists, skilled workers, and other townspeople than to those of slave masters or rural folk. The Brooklyn Excelsiors's tour had sparked the creation of several Baltimore clubs, while Washington, D.C., inaugurated the Potomac and National clubs in 1860. New Orleans experienced a baseball boom in 1859 when seven teams were started, and two more followed the next year. These early New Orleans nines at first used the Massachusetts rules, but by 1860 they all had switched to the NABBP regulations. In 1860 Kentucky boasted four clubs in Louisville and one in Newport, while Missouri had five in St. Louis and one in St. Joseph. In Texas townball games were common in Galveston prior to the

Civil War, and the new railroad center of Houston produced a baseball club on April 11, 1861, with three 5:00 A.M. practice sessions per week!

By the spring of 1861 the regional diffusion of baseball suggested that it was well on its way to becoming the true "national pastime" of the United States, thereby achieving a distinction that sporting journalists had prematurely granted it during the late 1850s. It was also clear that the "New York game" was prevailing over its rivals. But why was the NABBP version reigning supreme? One answer is simple: both spectators and players favored its rules. To a modern eye, the New York variety seems more efficient and appealing, especially considering the symmetry of the diamond compared to the townball square. The containment of play by foul lines permitted spectators to crowd closer to the action and cut down the ground that fielders had to cover. Furthermore, the NABBP game was undoubtedly safer, simpler, and easier for adults to learn and master. Surely the older players must have preferred the force and tag rules for putouts, instead of the townball custom of throwing (or "burning") the ball at the runners. James D'Wolf Lovett's preference for the "New York game" was shared by many: "The pitching, instead of swift throwing, looked easy to hit, and the pitcher stood off so far, and then there was no danger of getting plugged with the ball while running bases; and the ball was so lively and could be batted so far!" Three outs to a side also seemed to be an improvement over the New England custom of "one-out, all-out," permitting more action, more base runners, and hence more tension and drama. Nine innings brought the game to a conclusion within three hours, while many Massachusetts matches failed to reach a deciding one hundred runs before nightfall.

Yet the Masachusetts game and other variants of townball also had their good points and excitement, such as overhand pitching and the fly rule, later adopted by the NABBP and its successors. In fact, even as the New York game spread across America, several townball players and clubs remained loyal to their premodern form of ball. In Newark, New Jersey, the Knickerbocker Antiquarians remained true to their time-honored game. In Wisconsin one old timer much preferred the rule that allowed plugging base runners with balls. He criticized the New York game as "indolent, sickly, puerile, effeminate and disgusting to behold," condemning the new pastime as nothing more than a " 'yaller kivered' game to suit the shiftlessness of the age." Rule differences thus provide only part of the reason why the "New York game" won out over its rivals.

A better explanation may be found in the "urban imperialism" of the great city on the Hudson. During the middle decades of the nineteenth century, New York extended its economic influence throughout the west and south via its monumental transportation network of canals, railroads, and steamships. New York traders and bankers were active in attracting business toward their home city, and in doing so they established contacts with many strangers who came under their influence. At the same time the city was becoming a cultural center and a major threat to Boston as the leading literary and communication headquarters. Its sporting weeklies, as previously emphasized, also played a significant role in promoting New York baseball. Wherever New York businessmen and newspapers appeared, they carried with them their local sport. Thus it was not surprising to find baseball thriving in those cities where New Yorkers were active: Baltimore, St. Louis, New Orleans, Chicago, Washington, D.C., and San Francisco. More significantly, in many of these communities sportsmen imitated the men from Manhattan and Brooklyn by naming their clubs after the famous Atlantic, Excelsior, Eagle, and Empire clubs. Even Boston and Philadelphia came under the New York baseball influence as they fell further behind in population and commercial power. Thus, just as New York was defeating its major trade rivals and strengthening its position as the largest and most powerful city in the United States, it was also exporting and promoting its native sport as the American national pastime— an entertaining product that it marketed extremely well. There were certainly many men in smaller communities who looked to the big city for leadership, even as they may have resented its dominance. In contrast, Philadelphia and Boston were not as influential in the hinterlands, and their styles of ball play were not as attractive and could not compete with the game from Gotham.

Battlefront

I n the spring of 1861, baseball players in dozens of American cities and towns prepared their minds, bodies, and grounds for another brilliant season of play. But the news from Fort Sumter, South Carolina, sent shock waves throughout the sporting world. The beginning of four terrible years of civil war had important short- and long-term repercussions for baseball. The game became a feature of military life, and it took on new meanings in the context of war. Observers of American sporting life stressed the analogy between team sports and battle, urging the former as training for the latter. Thousands of players enlisted in regiments and competed in camp-grounds on makeshift playing fields as they awaited combat on bat-tlefields. In the course of time a few Confederate and Union prison-ers of war were even allowed to indulge in ball games to keep them active and to help them pass the long hours of incarceration as they awaited repatriation.

The sporting press of the late 1850s and early 1860s fre-quently pointed out the parallels between America's first team sports and war. In wrapping up its review of the 1857 season, using meta-phors that would too soon prove to be realities, the *Clipper* remarked that the players "will be compelled to lay by their weapons of war, enter into winter quarters, there to discuss and lay plans for the proper conducting of next season's campaign." Yet sportswriters were acutely aware of the crucial differences between play and mortal struggle. In March 1861 that journal hinted at the impending crisis:

"God forbid that any balls but those of the Cricket and Baseball field may be caught either on the fly or bound, and we trust that no arms but those of the flesh may be used to impel them, or stumps, but those of the wickets, injured by them." But three months later it remarked that "Cricket and Baseball clubs . . . are now enlisted in a different sort of exercise, the rifle or gun taking the place of the bat, while the play ball gives place to the leaden messenger of death. Men who have heretofore made their mark in friendly strife for superiority in various games, are now beating off the rebels who would dismember this glorious 'Union of States.' " In 1864 a Rochester reporter noted that "many of our first class players are now engaged in the 'grand match' against the rebellious 'side,' and already have made a 'score' which, in after years, they will be proud to look upon." That year a Union soldier, encamped with his regiment at Culpepper Court House in Virginia, reported that "if General Grant does not send them to have a match with Gen. Lee, they are willing to have another friendly match, but if he does, the blue coats think that the leaden balls will be much harder to stop than if thrown by friendly hands on the club grounds."

Although indulging in pastimes such as baseball might seem inappropriate in the emergency of wartime, several editorialists believed that team sports were useful in preparing men for more serious and deadly contests. The *Rochester Express* noted that with "the serious matter of war . . . upon our hands, . . . physical education and the development of muscle should be engendered" through baseball. In January 1862 the *Clipper* emphasized both the short and long term benefits of athletics in army camps. It reported: "Many officers who never before took a 'hand in' at any of our out-door games, are now among the leading spirits in the conduct of such matters; and the influence exerted thereby is spreading throughout the entire army. 'Young America' must have his sport, be he a soldier or a civilian, and with the leisure afforded him by a life of soldierly inactivity, he has ample time to indulge his sportive tastes." That writer predicted that "when the rebellion is crushed, and the Army of the Union mustered out of service, we will then have an abundance of the right sort of stuff with which to recruit our forces for the encouragement and practice of physical games and pastimes. As our friends are mustered out of the army, they will be mustered into the service for the peaceful pursuit of health giving exercises for the mind and body." Another commentator argued that baseball best promoted the health of the nation's young men, "for to excel in it, the player must be courageous, capable of enduring bodily fatigue, possess the judgment to conceive and the activity and skill to execute, and also the moral attributes of being courteous in manner and gentlemanly in language, besides having entire control of his temper." He noted: "These requisites are such as go to make up the first-rate soldier. Indeed, the practice of base ball is an admirable preliminary school for attaining many of the most important qualifications of a soldier, the endurance of bodily fatigue and the cultivation of activity of movement being two important elements."

Thousands of northern club members volunteered for service in the Union Army, while a few enlisted in the Confederate cause. Abraham G. Mills of Cincinnati, a future President of the National League and one of the chief perpetrators of the Doubleday-Cooperstown myth, packed a bat and ball with his army gear before reporting for military duty. He later recalled that he used his sporting equipment as much as his side arms. In late May of 1861 *Wilkes' Spirit of the Times* reported that the pitcher of the Union club of St. Louis planned to resign from his team to accept a commission in the Second Missouri Artillery after leading his team to victory in a championship match against a city rival, the Empire nine. According to the writer, "the boys console themselves with the hope that the balls he will pitch at the foes of his country's flag, may be as successful in putting down their insolent presumption, as were those pitched against his civil opponents yesterday, in humbling the more honest pride of the former Champions of Base Ball in St. Louis."

In New York City, where a stunning patriotic outburst reversed that metropolis' strong antebellum pro-southern sentiment, many sportsmen put ethnic and political differences aside to rally to the flag. The *Clipper* enthusiastically supported Lincoln's call for troops and published the names of enlistees, including ball players. It praised those who signed up, and urged others who were slower to act to follow their example. "Better join in, boys," it advised the slackers, "than be loafing the streets or hanging around bar-rooms, and thus show the people you have some noble traits that atone for whatever bad ones you get credit for." Otto W. Parisen, one of modern baseball's pioneer players and a member of the Knickerbockers of New York during the 1850s, received a commission in July 1861 as Captain in Company C and Quartermaster of the 9th Infantry Regiment, New York Volunteers. He survived the Battle of Antietam, was honorably discharged, and was commissioned again as a first lieutenant, Company F in the 122nd Infantry Regiment, New York Volunteers. He was mustered out in June 1865. G. S. Holt of the Henry Eckford club of Brooklyn was not so lucky. He was shot in August 1861 while returning to his camp with the Union Army, killed by "friendly fire" from another company on picket duty. Ninety-one members of Brooklyn's celebrated Excelsior club volunteered for the Union cause, but one of its first nine performers defected to the enemy. A. T. Pearsall, a successful physician, went over to the Confederate side in the winter of 1862–63. As a Brigade Surgeon in Richmond, Virginia he attended to a few Union prisoners, including some former fellow club members. He inquired about his former playmates, but when word of his whereabouts reached Brooklyn the Excelsior club expelled him.

Military authorities permitted recreation for soldiers at appropriate times and places between campaigns and during winter camps because it supplied diversion and proved useful. Thousands of energetic young men confined to army camps soon became bored with repetitive drills and chores. With plenty of free time on their hands and little to do outside of their training they naturally sought to amuse themselves. Their officers therefore permitted wholesome activities that would keep the recruits out of serious trouble. The U.S. Sanitary Commission recommended that "when practicable, amusements, sports, and gymnastic exercises should be favored amongst the men," and it listed baseball among the approved pastimes. Dr. Julian Chisolm, an author of a manual of surgery for the Confederate Army, suggested that while in camp "Temporary gymnasia might be established, and gymnastic exercise should be en-

31

5. Soldiers and ball players from Company G, 48th New York State Volunteers at Fort Pulaski, GA, c. 1862–63. This is the only known photograph of a baseball game played during the Civil War. Used with permission of the National Baseball Hall of Fame Library, Cooperstown, NY.

couraged as conductive to health, strength, agility, and address." He also specifically listed "manly play of ball" as part of a soldier's daily exercise schedule.

Officers on both sides encouraged sport on holidays, in winter camps, and also during breaks between drill sessions to relieve the boredom of camp life and to enliven the training period with activities that were enjoyable and exciting. They hoped to use athletics to motivate men for grueling drill sessions, to foster group cohesion and loyalty, and to upgrade the physical condition of recruits. The *Clipper* applauded the practice of games in camp, noting the "beneficial effect they have on the spirits and health, and how they tend to alleviate the monotony of camp life." It added: "They also lead to a wholesome rivalry between companies and regiments, and

6. Baseball Game at a Union Fort Garrison. This image depicts Union troops playing ball with sentries guarding earthworks and guns on the hill behind the ball field. The place and date are unknown. Used with permission of the Western Reserve Historical Society, Cleveland, OH.

augment the esprit du corps of the same, to an extent that to those who have not witnessed it would appear marvelous." George Lewis of Battery E, First Regiment of Rhode Island Light-Artillery recorded in his regimental history in December 1861: "Many of the boys had a revival of their school days in a game of ball. These amusements had much to do in preventing us from being homesick, and were productive, also, of health and happiness."

Northern and southern war diaries, memoirs, and regimental histories recount innumerable examples of recreational pastimes among Union and Confederate troops. The most popular were combative sports, especially boxing and wrestling matches, which were often used to settle personal disputes. Men from rural villages and counties naturally turned to familiar country amusements, such as fishing, hunting, target shooting, feats of strength, swimming, and horse races. Those who were more inclined to sedentary pursuits favored the quieter games of card playing and dominoes. Many soldiers preferred athletics, such as cricket, running and jumping contests, football (then primarily a kicking game, an early form of soccer), and baseball. In the miscellaneous category were a host of fun-filled frolics, including snowball encounters, greased pigs chases and greased pole climbing, sack and wheelbarrow races, and cock fights. As soldiers enjoyed their favorite amusements they were also exposed to unfamiliar forms of sports and games; some of them tried out these new pastimes (especially the New York version of baseball) and played them during the postwar period. Of course, as sport historian Patricia Millen has pointed out, baseball games were far less common in army camps than other simpler forms of amusement—especially card playing. When men did play ball, their matches tended to be informal contests within their own regiments, briefly noted in their diaries as part of the routine of a soldier's life.

Any discussion of the impact of baseball on northern and southern troops must begin with the theory that Albert G. Spalding expounded in his classic early history of the sport, *America's National Game*:

No human mind may measure the blessings conferred by the game of Base Ball on the soldiers of our Civil War. A National Game? Why, no country on the face of the earth ever had a form of sport with so clear a title to that distinction. Base Ball had been born in the brain of an American soldier. It received its baptism in bloody days of our Nation's direst danger. It had its early evolution when soldiers, North and South, were striving to forget their foes by cultivating, through this grand game, fraternal friendships with comrades in arms. It had its best development at the time when Southern soldiers, disheartened by distressing defeat, were seeking the solace of something safe and sane; at a time when Northern soldiers, flushed with victory, were yet willing to turn from fighting with bombs and bullets to playing with bat and ball. It was a panacea for the pangs of humiliation to the vanquished on the one side, and a sedative against the natural exuberance of victors on the other. It healed the wounds of war, and was balm to stinging memories of sword thrust and saber stroke. It served to fill the enforced leisure hours of countless thousands of men suddenly thrown out of employment. It calmed the restless spirits of men who, after four years of bitter strife, found themselves all at once in the midst of a monotonous era, with nothing at all to do.

And then, when true patriots of all sections were striving to forget that there had been a time of black and dismal war, it was a beacon, lighting their paths to a future of perpetual peace. And, later still, it was a medium through which the men who had worn the blue, found welcome to the cities of those who had worn the gray, and before the decade of the sixties had died the game of Base Ball helped all of us to "know no North, no South,"only remembering a reunited Nation, whose game it was henceforth to be forever.

It is easy to refute his reference to Abner Doubleday's alleged invention of baseball. But what about the remainder of his claims concerning the impact of baseball on the men at war? What exactly was the meaning of the sport in the context of the deadly conflict between North and South? Did it have the positive short- and long-term benefits on the victorious and vanquished troops as Spalding argues? Did the war really help to spread baseball to all regions, and was it a helpful agent of sectional reconciliation after the war? This and subsequent chapters will show that there is some truth to Spalding's assertions, although the consequences of the war for baseball were more complicated than he suggested.

As the historian Reid Mitchell has persuasively argued, the recruitment of northern soldiers and their commitment to the Union cause must be understood in the context of the values and institutions of their home communities, including rural villages, small towns, and urban neighborhoods in large cities. Local leaders raised companies and regiments; officers and common enlisted men generally knew each other quite well. Their companies were primarily military institutions, but they also resembled the private voluntary associations, including athletic clubs, that were so common in antebellum America. It is not surprising to find that the towns and cities most infected with the baseball fever of the period from 1857 to 1861 also produced the regiments that were most active on campground ball fields. Men who had joined baseball associations before

7. "Call for Volunteers." This image of ball players volunteering for military service reflects Albert G. Spalding's view of the link between patriotism and baseball during the Civil War. It was drawn around 1911, the date of the publication of Spalding's *America's National Game*. Used with permission of the New York Public Library. Photography Collection, Miriam and Ira D. Wallach Division of Art, Prints and Photographs, Astor, Lenox, and Tilden Foundations.

the war were accustomed to wearing club uniforms as they took on the role of athlete. When they joined the army they adopted a martial life and clothing. Then when they competed in baseball matches they played both roles. Of course not all recruits were dedicated soldiers and healthy, talented athletes. As George T. Stevens of the 77th Regiment, New York Volunteers remembered: "Each regiment had its share of disease and desertion; each had its ball-players and its singers, its story-tellers and its merry fellows."

Most of the baseball players who enlisted in Civil War armies came from the northeast (especially Manhattan and Brooklyn), but all regions contributed ball players turned soldiers, including the Confederacy. Soldiers played the New York and Massachusetts versions of the game, along with premodern types of townball. To enjoy their practice sessions and matches they improvised makeshift grounds, constructed rudimentary equipment, and arranged contests both in camp and perilously close to enemy positions. Men from Manhattan, Brooklyn, and upstate New York naturally dominated many contests. In October 1861 a "bold Soldier boy" sent the *Clipper* an account of a baseball game played by prominent Brooklyn club members on the parade ground of the "Mozart Regiment, now in Secessia." He was eager to report the sports news to civilians on the home front, "lest you might imagine that the 'sacred soil' yields only to the tramp of the soldier; that its hills echo only the booming gun, and the dying shriek." The men, he explained, were "engaged in their old familiar sports, totally erasing from their minds the all absorbing topic of the day." Mills remembered that on Christmas Day, 1862, before a crowd of 40,000 soldiers at Hilton Head, South Carolina, a team from the 165th New York Volunteer Infantry, Duryea's Zouaves, played a match against a picked nine from other Union regiments. Nicholas E. Young, later a president of the National League, was a cricketer from a town in upstate New York who played his favorite sport in the army near White Oak Church, Virginia, in the early spring of 1863. In that year he switched his allegiance from cricket to baseball after the 27th New York Regiment organized a club. According to Mason Whiting Tyler, during that season ball games were "all the rage now in the Army of the Potomac," and his camp was "alive with ball-players, almost every street having its game." George T. Stevens of the New York Volunteers remembered that when he was at Falmouth, Virginia that year "there were many excellent players in the different regiments, and it was common for the ball-players of one regiment or brigade to challenge another regiment or brigade." He added: "These matches were watched by great crowds of soldiers with intense interest." When the Fourteenth Regiment returned to Brooklyn in June 1864 a comrade in arms from the Thirteenth Regiment wrote to the *Brooklyn Daily Eagle*: "Among the returned heroes of our gallant Fourteenth are some well known ball players, who, while devoted to the use of more deadly weapons, have not forgotten the use of bat or ball, as the many games played

8. "On Tented Fields—in Prison Pens." This image was prepared for
Spalding's *America's National Game*, published in 1911. The American flag in
the center links two views of troops playing baseball on a camp field and
also inside a prison yard. Used with permission of the New York Public
Library. Photography Collection, Miriam and Ira D. Wallach Division of Art,
Prints and Photographs, Astor, Lenox, and Tilden Foundations.

by them during their three years service will prove." He proposed an "amalgamated match" between the two regiments to inaugurate a new ball ground in Coney Island. The Star Club of Brooklyn graciously offered their practice field to the men of the Fourteenth Regiment to help them organize a team at home.

When New Englanders competed among themselves they often played by the rules of the "Massachusetts game," but when they faced New Yorkers they sometimes observed the NABBP regulations. (Newspaper accounts generally did not specify which type of the sport was played in army camp games.) John G. B. Adams of the Nineteenth Massachusetts Regiment recalled that while he was encamped in Falmouth in early 1863 a "base ball fever broke out." Enlisted men and officers played "the old-fashioned game, when a man running the bases must be hit by the ball to be declared out." After a short while Adams's Regiment challenged the Seventh Regiment of Michigan to play a game for sixty dollars a side. The Massachusetts men prevailed, and the prize money was spent on a supper for players on both sides and their guests. Adams declared: "It was a grand time, and all agreed that it was nicer to play *base* than *minie* [bullet] ball." That June a correspondent to the *Clipper* reported a match following the Massachusetts game rules played for $50 a side between Massachusetts's Eleventh Regiment and the Twenty-Sixth of Pennsylvania. He noted: "We have four clubs in our brigade, and there are several more in the division."

Confederate troops played townball as well as more modern versions of the game in their army camps. In November 1861 the *Charleston Mercury* of South Carolina reported that Confederate troops were stuck in soggy camps near Centreville, Fairfax County, Virginia. Heavy rains created miserably wet conditions so that "even the baseball players find the green sward in front of the camp, too boggy for their accustomed sport." Bell Wiley, in *The Life of Johnny Reb*, cites one anecdote of ball playing in the Twenty-fourth Alabama Regiment as Joe Johnston's southern troops watched for General William Sherman's movements. But Wiley also states that baseball games were common in practically every regiment of the Confederacy. Because southerners had a much harder time than their northern counterparts in obtaining good bats and balls, they generally had to make do with rudimentary home made equipment. In Wiley's words: "the bat might be a board, a section of some farmer's fence rail, or a slightly trimmed hickory limb; the pellet might be nothing better than a yarn-wrapped walnut; but enthusiasm would be so great as to make the camp reverberate with the cheers and taunts of participants, if not of spectators." In early April of 1862 the *Charleston Mercury* remarked that "every volunteer who has been in service, has realized the tedium of camp life. . . . there is waste time, which might be used advantageously at such manly exercises as cricket, baseball, foot ball, quoit pitching, etc." That paper lamented the shortage of sporting goods available for the men and called for hardware dealers to supply quoits (flat iron rings tossed as in horseshoes) and also cricket and baseball bats. "For want of such things," it concluded, "the time of the soldier is mainly spent playing cards."

In *America's National Game* Spalding recounted a rumor "that in Virginia, in the long campaign before Richmond, at periods when active hostilities were in abeyance, a series of games was played between picked nines from Federal and Confederate forces." Although Spalding reported no direct evidence of those contests, he did cite "cases where good-natured badinage had been exchanged between Union and Confederate soldiers on the outposts of opposing armies in the field." John G. B. Adams of the Nineteenth Massachusetts recalled that early in 1863 several men of the Union army encamped at Falmouth played baseball and also watched Confederates play games across a river. He wrote: "We would sit on the bank and watch their games, and the distance was so short we could understand every movement and would applaud good plays." While he did not mention any Union-Confederate contests, he did observe southerners fishing and throwing part of their catch to northern boys. He also stated that "our men and theirs met in the river and exchanged papers, tobacco and coffee and were on the best of terms." In a history of American sport, Wells Twombly recounted that members of Stonewall Jackson's second brigade were chasing a hare when they encountered a group of Yankees. The story goes that after the northern troops waved their hands to signify that they carried no weapons they engaged in a baseball game. Their match intrigued the Confederates, who then expressed a desire to learn the New York rules. It is a nice tale, but unfortunately Twombly did not cite any primary source to support it.

Numerous accounts of baseball in army camps highlight the role that officers had in encouraging, facilitating and often even participating in games. It appears likely that they did so because they recognized the beneficial effects of the sport on their men, but it is also undoubtedly true that they simply enjoyed the play. Charles E. Davis, Jr. of the Thirteenth Massachusetts Volunteers related that when his Regiment was in Virginia in early May 1862 they were surprised during a match when General George L. Hartsuff rode by, "got off his horse and requested permission to catch behind the bat, informing us there was nothing he enjoyed so much." Although he stayed only a few minutes, he impressed Davis "without in the least sacrificing his dignity or suggesting the lessening of his discipline, the cords of which we already noticed were tightening." In January 1864, while in winter quarters in Mountain Run, Thomas M. Aldrich of Battery A, First Regiment, Rhode Island Light Artillery participated in a contest in honor of General William Hays, "who had sent to Washington for balls and bats to enable us to play to good advantage." He explained: "When the general and his wife came galloping into camp, with a number of officers and ladies, our captain went out to greet them and said 'Ah! general, I suppose you would like to see the battery on drill.' The general quickly replied 'No; I want to see them play ball, which they can do better than any men I ever saw'." General Hays returned with his wife a few weeks later to watch another game. At about the same time near Brandy Station, Virginia Captain Lemuel A. Abbott of the Tenth Regiment Vermont Volunteer Infantry played in a match against a side of non-commissioned officers for an oyster dinner, with his team victorious.

Sometimes the war disrupted these pastimes, which were supposed to divert the soldiers' attention from the dangers and possible death awaiting them. In the spring of 1862 during a game between the Fifty-Seventh and Sixty-Ninth Regiments of New York

Jacob Cole was lying on the ground watching the match when he heard a "rumbling noise." When Cole and his friend stood up they heard nothing, but when they put their ears to the ground Cole told his friend that "our boys are fighting." He remembered: "Hardly had I spoken before orders came to report to our regiments at once. So the ball game came to a sudden stop never to resume." Generally soldiers sported within the relative security of their encampments, though sometimes they violated army regulations and competed outside the fortifications and beyond the line of pickets. George H. Putnam remembered a contest among Union troops in Texas that was aborted by a surprise enemy assault: "Suddenly there came a scattering fire of which the three fielders caught the brunt; the center field was hit and was captured, the left and right field managed to get into our lines." The northern soldiers repulsed the Confederate attack, "but we had lost not only our center field but . . . . the only baseball in Alexandria."

Baseball historians have long asserted that during the Civil War prisoners played the sport in both northern and southern camps, and also that matches played in those institutions introduced modern forms of the game to novices and helped with the cultural diffusion of baseball after the return of peace. Fragmentary evidence does support these conclusions, although it must be remembered that premodern versions of baseball were well known in all sections of the nation prior to the war. It appears that ball play was common in several prisons, especially during the first two years of the conflict. But as conditions deteriorated after 1862, especially in the south, athletic contests occurred less frequently. Union and Confederate prisons all experienced increasingly crowded and unsanitary conditions, with inadequate food, clothing, and shelter. Poor diets, oppressive heat in the summer and freezing cold in the winter, rampant disease, lack of sufficient space, and in some cases brutal treatment by guards all made strenuous physical activities highly problematic for the inmates. To pass long hours of incarceration, however, men did play checkers, chess, and card games and gamble with rations or what little money and wealth they possessed. There are even accounts of musical balls when half of the participants dressed themselves in blanket skirts and filled out formal dance cards. Officers tended to be better educated and in some institutions, such as that on Johnson's Island, Ohio, organized debating societies and classes in French, dancing, and music. Wrestling and boxing matches often resulted naturally from personal encounters, especially when conditions were the worst. Baseball matches became special events that a few privileged prisoners enjoyed and many others watched when circumstances permitted.

The two prisons that featured the most extensive baseball playing were the camps at Salisbury, North Carolina, and Johnson's Island, in Lake Erie near Sandusky, Ohio. A well-known illustration and several diary accounts document the participation of inmates in the sport at the Salisbury institution. Otto Boetticher was a commercial artist from New York City who enlisted in the 68th New York Volunteers in 1861 at the age of 45. He was captured in 1862 and wound up at Salisbury before being exchanged for a Confederate captain on September 30th. His drawing presents an idealized, pastoral view of a match in a setting that more closely resembled the Elysian Fields in Hoboken than a jail yard. Charles Carroll Gray was a doctor who was held at Salisbury from May 17 to July 28, 1862. In his diary he recorded that July 4th was "celebrated with music, reading of the Declaration of Independence, and sack and foot races in the afternoon, and also a baseball game." Indeed, he recalled that baseball was played nearly every day that the weather permitted. William J. Crossley, a sergeant in Company C, Second Rhode Island Infantry Volunteers, was captured at the Battle of Bull Run, July 21, 1861. He was transported to camps at Richmond, Virginia, and Tuscaloosa, Alabama before winding up at Salisbury on March 13, 1862. In his memoir he described a baseball match at Salisbury that spring between sides of men previously held in New Orleans and Tuscaloosa. He recalled that the "great game of baseball" generated "as much enjoyment to the Rebs as the Yanks, for they came in hundreds to see the sport." He added: "I have seen more smiles today on their oblong faces than before since I came to Rebeldom, for they have been the most doleful looking set of men I ever saw, and that Confederate gray uniform really adds to their mournful appear-

9. "Union Prisoners at Salisbury, N.C." Otto Boetticher drew this idealized image of union troops playing baseball in a Confederate prison camp. He was a commercial artist from New York City who was captured in 1862 and released in September of that year, before conditions in that prison deteriorated significantly. This illustration was published in 1863. Library of Congress, Prints and Photographs Division.

ance." The game ended in a draw, eleven runs each, but "the factory fellows were skunked [shut out] three times, and we [from the Tuscaloosa prison] but twice." Another commentator "regretted that we have no official report of the match-games played in Salisbury between the New Orleans and Tuscaloosa boys, resulting in the triumph of the latter." He explained that "the cells of the Parish Prison were unfavorable to the development of the *skill of the 'New Orleans Nine.'* " Crossley was released that summer as part of a general exchange of prisoners, rejoined his old regiment in October, and fought again at campaigns at Fredericksburg, Gettysburg, Chancellorsville, the Wilderness, Spottsylvania, and Cold Harbor.

There is also evidence that some of the prison guards at Salisbury joined in or at least watched the action on the diamond. Josephus Clarkson was a Boston ship chandler's apprentice before the war who was incarcerated at Salisbury. In his diary he recalled that the inmates preferred to follow the New York rules rather than the townball regulations since the latter game allowed fielders to "plug" base runners with the ball to record an out. He remembered that a pitcher from Texas was removed from one game after "badly laming" several prisoners. Clarkson wrote that "the game of baseball had been played much in the South, but many of them [the guards] had never seen the sport devised by Mr. Cartwright." His side had to politely inform their captors "that we would no longer play with a man who could not continue to observe the rules." Adolphus Magnum, a Confederate chaplain who visited the prison in 1862, wrote that a few inmates "ran like schoolboys to the play ground and were soon joining in high glee in a game of ball." He added: "Others . . . sat down side by side with the prison officials and witnessed the sport."

Through 1862 Salisbury prison was not filled to capacity, and the decent supply of food, frequent prisoner exchanges, and opportunities for recreation made life reasonably tolerable for most of the inmates. But conditions deteriorated significantly from late 1862 through the end of the war—especially over the last few months because of overcrowding, severe winter weather, a breakdown of prison control, and shortages of shelter, food, medicine, and fuel. Approximately one-quarter of Salisbury's total prison population of fifteen thousand perished within its walls, with most of the victims dying over the last months of its existence. There is no direct evidence of ball playing there during that period, and given the horrific conditions and poor health of the inmates it is unlikely that they participated in any athletic games from 1863 until the surviving prisoners were liberated through an exchange agreement in February 1865.

After 1862 Johnson's Island prison in Ohio was restricted to officers. Conditions there were generally better than at most other camps, in part because of the rank of the inmates and also because its average prison population was only about two thousand five hundred. Although the southerners suffered from lack of food and especially the intense cold in the winter, during the summer months the weather was fine for baseball. William Peel of the 11th Mississippi Infantry Regiment was captured at the Battle of Gettysburg and sent to Johnson's Island. In July he noted in his diary that an inmate was injured when a bat flew out of a hitter's hands during a game of ball.

Colonel D. R. Hundley was a native of Alabama and a graduate of Harvard Law School who married a daughter of a Virginia gentleman with real estate holdings in the suburbs of Chicago. Hundley moved to a house on the lake shore north of the city in 1856, but spent several winters in his home state. A supporter of Stephen Douglas for the presidency in 1860, after Lincoln's election he relocated to Alabama and joined the Thirty-First Alabama Infantry in the Confederate Army. He was captured by Union forces in June 1864. In his diary he recorded great excitement on August 27, 1864 over a baseball match between the Southron [sic] and Confederate clubs, "the former having for their colors white shirts, and the latter red shirts." He wrote: "During the progress of the game, nearly all the prisoners looked on with eager interest, and bets were made freely among those who had the necessary cash, and who were given to such practices; and very soon the crowd was pretty nearly equally divided between the partisans of the white shirts and those of the red shirts, and a real rebel yell went up from the one side or the other at every success of the chosen colors. The Yankees themselves outside the prison yard seemed to be not indifferent spectators of the game, but crowded the house-tops, and looked on with as much interest almost as did the rebels themselves." Peel recalled that there were several hundred dollars wagered on that match by the clubs and outsiders, in which "The Southerners beat the Confederates very badly: the Rounds standing nineteen to eleven."

Another account of the August 27th contest by Lt. M. McNamara lists Charlie H. Pierce as captain and catcher of the "Southern" nine (composed of those below the rank of captain), which defeated the Confederate team (made up of men of higher rank). McNamara estimated the crowd of spectators at about 3,000, including prisoners, officers, and citizens of Sandusky, Ohio. He also stated that "so apprehensive were the prison officials that the game was gotten up for the purpose of covering an attempt to break out, that they had the slides of the port holes drawn back and the guns prepared for action." A local newspaper published a detailed and favorable account of the game, but apparently some radical northern newspapers were highly critical of the prison's commanding officer for permitting the prisoners such recreation. According to McNamara, "their malicious efforts were successful, the commander was removed, and the amusement of the unhappy prisoners, for the time being, cut off." But not all was fun and games for Hundley, Peel, and their comrades. Hundley described the great hunger men suffered that drove many to hunt for rats to eat. He even recorded the founding of a "Rat Club, (which is now a recognized institution, on an equal footing with our Chess Club, our Base-Ball Club, Cricket Club, and numerous others.)"

Prisoners also played the game in other camps. In a *Collier's Weekly* article dated May 8, 1909, Will Irwin wrote about New Orleans boys who "carried base balls in their knapsacks" and "found themselves in a Federal prison stockade on the Mississippi," perhaps the one at Rock Island. He explained: "They formed a club. Confederate prisoners from Georgia and South Carolina watched them, got the hang of it and organized for rivalry. In the East and West Series that followed the West won triumphantly by unrecorded scores."

Considering the widespread popularity of various forms of premodern baseball and the emergence of the "New York game" during the 1850s, it is not surprising that many soldiers carried bats and balls in their knapsacks during the Civil War. Officers endorsed the playing of the sport as a wholesome and beneficial relief from the repetitive military drills and the overall monotony of camp life. Ball matches helped recruits pass the days and months between battles, and these spirited contests also amused inmates in Union and Confederate prisons. But while the men in uniform kept the game going in the midst of war, the fate of baseball back on the home front was uncertain. Public opinion in the New York City region, Boston, Philadelphia, and smaller towns and rural communities would determine whether civilian players and club officers would suspend their activity until the return of peace, or whether they would advance the game to new levels of acceptance and participation.

3

Home Front

While baseball enthusiasts enjoyed their favorite sport in army camps, the game suffered some understandable setbacks on the home front. Yet the sport endured the trials of civil war remarkably well, persisting and even progressing under trying circumstances. The growth of the game during these years is truly remarkable—a testament to the powerful momentum that the sport had built up between 1857 and 1860 in several northeastern cities. Baseball had already begun to cast its magical spell over the sporting fraternity and thousands of other residents in many major metropolitan centers. Its acceptance by military officials as a wholesome recreation for their troops gave it greater legitimacy, and its popularity among civilians further secured its place in the nation's cultural landscape. Although many patriotic players enlisted in service to the Union, others chose to delay or evade their calls to duty. It appears that those who remained at home and played ball were not dishonored or stigmatized to any significant degree, especially compared to their counterparts in twentieth century wars.

Despite the disruptions of war, the early 1860s marked a critical period in the evolution of the national pastime. Those years witnessed the triumph of the New York style of play in Boston and Philadelphia, major rule revisions by the National Association of Base Ball Players, and the growth of commercialism and even some professionalism in baseball. City championship matches and intercity tours boosted the popularity of the game, as did sporting weeklies which chronicled the game's growth. Club officials could not ignore the carnage on battlefields, and they scheduled special benefit contests with gate receipts dedicated to the U.S. Sanitary Commission, which provided care for injured soldiers. As the war drew to a close, some disturbing trends also appeared that would plague baseball for years to come. They included ill will among club members over championship matches, gambling and charges of corruption, and occasional interference from spectators, ranging from heckling to the rare riot.

While the shadow of war certainly reached the urban centers of the north, it only slightly dimmed the bright lights of the world of leisure, especially in the largest cities. To be sure, the first year or two of civil war severely tested the people of those communities, but by 1863 the prosperity produced by wartime spending enabled many civilians to enjoy more comfortable and even affluent lifestyles. The upper classes of financiers, merchants, factory owners, and professionals crowded into hotels, theaters, operas, and shops. In October 1863 an editorial in the *New York Herald* subtitled "The Age of Shoddy" described the impact of the war on the new rich:

> This war has entirely changed the American character. The lavish profusion in which the old Southern cotton aristocracy used to indulge is completely eclipsed by the dash, parade and magnificence of the new Northern shoddy aristocracy of this period. The individual who makes the most money—no matter how—and spends the most money—no matter for what—is considered the greatest man. To be extravagant is to be fashionable. These facts sufficiently account for the immense and brilliant audiences at the opera and the theatres; and until the final crash comes such audiences will undoubtedly continue.

A month later the *London Times* observed: "This war has brought the levity of the American character out in bald relief. There is something saddening, indeed revolting, in the high glee, real or affected, with which the people here look upon what ought to be, at any rate, a grievous national calamity. The indulgence in every variety of pleasure, luxury, and extravagance is simply shocking." In June 1864 the *New York Independent* proclaimed: "Who at the North would ever think of war, if he had not a friend in the army, or did not read the newspapers? Go into Broadway, and we will show you what is meant by the word 'extravagance.' Ask Stewart about the demand for camel's-hair shawls, and he will say 'monstrous.' Ask Tiffany what kind of diamonds and pearls are called for. He will answer 'the prodigious,' 'as near hen's-egg size as possible,' 'price no object.' "

The wartime prosperity in several northeastern cities and the ability of many men to avoid military service both contributed greatly to a revival of sports in those communities by 1863. Baseball especially regained much of its early momentum, while cricket did not. There were ample numbers of skilled players to field several first class clubs in Boston, New York City, Brooklyn, Newark, and Philadelphia and multitudes of fans (including many gamblers) to watch them compete. Newspaper editors realized that their readers were interested in accounts of exciting matches along with battlefield news, and they recruited sportswriters to fill columns with detailed stories on major and even minor matches.

As the war raged on, all classes indulged in a variety of sports and amusements. The elites did have to curtail their yachting, but they also continued to patronize horse racing for both trotters and thoroughbreds. Remarkably, a group of New Yorkers led by the celebrated bare-knuckle boxer and gambler John Morrissey and a few blue blood aristocrats founded a racetrack at Saratoga Springs in 1863. Middle and lower class clerks, shop keepers, artisans, workers, teachers, students, journalists, and other urban dwellers also had their more low brow amusements during the war years. These included popular concerts, plays, minstrel shows, circuses, and more exotic exhibits of wild beasts and freaks of nature. For athletics they turned to baseball, cricket, and gymnastics (introduced by German turners), and they also patronized pub sports such as billiards, bowling, and quoits. In winter ice skating was all the rage, especially in the newly opened Central Park in Manhattan, where ladies were welcome and baseball on ice was a novelty. Bare-knuckle prize fights were illegal but still attracted a mix of gentlemen, gamblers, and workers. Blood sports such as cockfights and dog fights drew mostly a clientele of bettors and workers, as middle class animal rights advocates were beginning their crusade to ban these brutal contests.

In the world of sports the events of 1861 and 1862 proved to be very disruptive, but by 1863 there were signs of revival for athletics in general and baseball in particular. Initially, with so many sportsmen marching off to war, and with civilian anxieties focused on battlefield news, interest in playful contests naturally waned. Two months after the first shots at Fort Sumter, a *Clipper* editorial on the impact of the war on New York City life noted that the conflict "has knocked sports out of business, and thrown a damper on every little amusement we heretofore enjoyed so well." At summer's end in 1861 that journal described the dullness of New York's sporting life: "many of our . . . friends have enlisted in the defence of the Union, while those that remained . . . lacked the spirit to indulge in those recreations so rife among us in former seasons."

Proof of the disruptive effects of the war on baseball appeared in the disbanding of many clubs, the reduction in the number of first-nine contests among the best players in each club, and the drop in attendance at the annual conventions of the National Association. For example, the famed Atlantics of Brooklyn did not inaugurate the 1861 season until August 11th and played only seven matches that year, compared to sixteen in 1860. Their arch rivals, the Excelsiors, did not play a single formal match against another club that year, with slim attendance on their grounds on practice days. Joseph Leggett's departure with the Thirteenth Regiment dealt a severe blow to the Excelsiors, because, according to the *Clipper*, he was "the life and soul of the club." Ninety of his fellow club members also enlisted under the colors of the Union Army. James D'Wolf Lovett of Boston recalled: "In 1861 the Civil War burst and many baseball plans were disarranged thereby, some of the players enlisting upon the first call for troops; and during the war's progress upwards of fifty members of Boston's clubs were to be found in Uncle Sam's ranks."

Fresh calls for troops from Washington, D.C., throughout the war further depleted baseball nines. In 1862 the two leading teams in Newark, New Jersey almost entirely suspended play because so many of their men enlisted. In Detroit, Michigan the Early Risers and Franklins disappeared, while the Brother Jonathans skipped the 1861 season but were back in the field the next year. The Detroit Base Ball Club played only one regular match in 1861, as many of its members took on important civilian responsibilities in the war effort. As late as the summer of 1864 fears of a renewed Confederate invasion of Pennsylvania moved that state's Governor to call for thirty thousand more militia. That particular recruitment had a direct impact on a series of intercity matches between Philadelphia's and Brooklyn's premier teams, depriving the former of key players.

But after an initial setback baseball generated a surprising amount of enthusiasm during the war era. In part this was due to the love of the game displayed by boys and college students who were not yet old enough or ready for military service. But more important were the featured contests of adult nines composed of men who did not volunteer for the Union or who were not drafted into the army. In certain hotbeds of baseball—especially New York City, Brooklyn, and Newark, New Jersey—there was continuing criticism of Lincoln's wartime policies. While there is little concrete evidence that links ball players with Democratic politicians who advocated compromises with the Confederacy, one may speculate that some of these athletes were less than enthusiastic about risking their lives for the Union. On the other hand, in Philadelphia there were several leading players who served short-term tours of duties with regiments and who also competed in major matches for their home town clubs.

New York City remained the center of the baseball universe, and there it rebounded quickly. In its review of the 1861 season in the New York region, the *Clipper* reported that "the game has too strong a foothold in popularity to be frowned out of favor by the lowering brow of 'grim-visaged war,' and if any proof was needed that our national game is a fixed institution of the country, it would be found in the fact, that it has flourished through such a year of adverse circumstances as those that have marked the season of 1861." In the fall of 1861 the Atlantics and the Mutuals split a home and home series, but the feature contest of that season was a special event that matched select nines from the rival cities of Brooklyn and Manhattan. With the *Clipper* offering a silver ball as a trophy to the club whose men scored the greatest number of runs, the Brooklynites defeated the men from Gotham, with the Atlantics carrying off the prize ball. The game, played on October 21, drew thousands of spectators, even though several newspapers had reported that the contest would be postponed—perhaps to diminish an event promoted by a rival periodical. That year the Continental Base Ball Club also planned to give a silver ball to the champion club of the NABBP, but the outbreak of the war made it impossible to arrange the proper series to determine a champion club. In 1862 the Continentals revived their offer, and scheduled a championship series between the Atlantics and the Eckfords, the net proceeds going to the Brooklyn Sanitary Commission, earmarked for sick and wounded soldiers. The mania for the game had returned to the New York City metropolitan region, and the fervor would only intensify during the remaining years of intersectional strife.

The "Massachusetts Game" still remained quite popular among army men, but on the home front the New York version predominated. It gained momentum in New England in July of 1862 when a tour by the Brooklyn Excelsiors stirred great interest among Boston's sporting fraternity. James D'Wolf Lovett, one of the founders of the Lowell junior club, recalled that the celebrated Excelsiors "were in their prime at this time, and, being the first New York club to visit Boston, created much excitement. . . . Ball players from all parts of New England came to see them play, and our eyes were opened to many things." Lovett paid close attention to Jim Creighton's underhand wrist movement in his fast and accurate pitching, and he later imitated the famed Excelsior's delivery of the ball. Before a large crowd on July 10th the Excelsiors routed the home town Bowdoins 41–15, and the next day they easily defeated a picked nine of players from the Tri-Mountain and Lowell nines, 39–13. A correspondent to the *Clipper* reported that during the war four clubs in the Boston vicinity (the Tri-Mountain, Bowdoin, Lowell, and Shawmut) had adopted the NABBP rules, and others were expected to follow soon. In 1863 *Wilkes' Spirit* grandly proclaimed that "the National Association game has won for itself the almost unanimous approval of all who take any interest in the sport; and the clubs who adopt any other style of playing are every day, becoming 'small by degrees, and beautifully less.' "

In October 1864 John A. Lowell of Boston offered a silver ball as a prize for the championship series of New England played on Boston Common between the Tri-Mountains, Lowells, and the Osceola club of Portland, Maine, with the Lowells victorious. In reporting the results of these games *Wilkes' Spirit* credited Lowell with "the great increasing interest taken in baseball, especially in Boston and vicinity." It added: "Several of the old Massachusetts clubs are changing their style to the national game." In March 1865 that journal published a brief history and the rules of the "Massachusetts game," but added an editorial comment that "the Massachusetts and still more ancient style of playing familiar to any school-boy, called 'town ball,' will soon become obsolete."

The most striking evidence of baseball's capacity to flourish amid the adversity of war occurred in Philadelphia, where it overtook both townball and cricket during the early 1860s. Of the dozen local clubs organized at that time, the most active were the Olympic, Athletic, Mercantile, and Keystone. The Olympics, founded as a townball team in 1833, claimed to be the oldest ball club in the nation. Their members, mostly businessmen who played the game as "an innocent amusement that cannot injure them mentally," switched to baseball in 1859. Although the Olympic first nine competed for city championship honors for a few years, by 1864 the club had retired from major matches, and many of its men reverted back to their time-honored pastime of townball. Their arch rivals were the Athletics, several of whom were vocalists who were also attached to the Handel and Hayden Musical Society. These gentlemen also began with townball in 1859 but changed to baseball in April 1860. A nasty exchange of letters published in the *Clipper* during the spring of 1862 attests to the bad feeling between these two clubs, as a few of their members took turns attacking each other's organization over arrangements for playing grounds, disputed decisions by umpires, and personal conduct by participants. The Mercantiles were prominent gentlemen and leading businessmen who played mostly intrasquad and practice games for recreation. The Keystones ranked second to the Athletics by 1864, with nearly two hundred members and three good nines.

During the war years the Athletics developed into the dominant team in Philadelphia, and by 1865 its first nine was challenging the leading clubs of New York City and Brooklyn for championship honors. Its president, Colonel Thomas Fitzgerald, was editor of Philadelphia's *City Item* and a well-known dramatist and art critic who campaigned actively for Abraham Lincoln in the presidential elections of 1860 and 1864. Among its star players in the early 1860s were two men who were prominent cricketers but earned fame in baseball before retiring in the 1870s. Tom Pratt's pitching so impressed the Brooklyn Atlantics that they recruited him from the Athletics in the middle of the 1863 season. His delivery of the ball was fast but straight and he earned a reputation for deceiving both the batsman and the umpire at the same time. When Pratt defected to the Atlantics he was replaced by James Dickinson (Dick) McBride, who began his career as an outfielder and shortstop before becoming one of the premier hurlers of his era. Unlike Pratt he remained loyal to the Athletics for fifteen years as an amateur and then a professional in the National Association of Professional Base Ball Players. He closed out his illustrious career with a final season with Boston in 1876.

During the Civil War era baseball survived and occasionally showed signs of vitality in the West, Washington, D.C., the South, and even Canada. Michigan's clubs included nines from Detroit, Kalamazoo, Dowagiac, Ypsilanti, Ann Arbor, Howell, Jackson, Monroe, Niles, Marshall, Concord, Chelsea, Dexter, and Lodi. A contingent of "Rocky Mountain Boys" played the "New York game" in Denver. Near the end of the ordeal the nation's capital experienced a baseball revival, thanks in part to resident New Yorkers who worked in the Treasury Department and played for the National and Union clubs on the grounds at the rear of the White House. In the South the conquest of New Orleans in April 1862 brought baseball back into Dixie. New York style baseball also increased its presence in Canada during this period. The Young Canadians of Woodstock and the Maple Leafs of Hamilton in Ontario pioneered the sport in their country, and joined with two other clubs to found the Canadian Base Ball Association in 1864. That fall the Young Canadians met the Brooklyn Atlantics for "the championship of the American continent" at the Rochester (N.Y.) State Fair. The Atlantics crushed the foreign challengers, yet the event sparked greater interest in baseball north of the border.

Intercity tours of clubs from Philadelphia, Newark, Manhattan, and Brooklyn from 1862 through 1864 strengthened the baseball fraternity of New York, New Jersey, and Pennsylvania and promoted the NABBP. The sporting press devoted significant space to these series and encouraged club officials to make all necessary arrangements for travel and accommodations to ensure comfort and good feeling among all parties. For the most part harmony and good sportsmanship prevailed during these challenges, but there were exceptions that will be examined later. In most cases the hosts scheduled elaborate pre- and post-game entertainment. To cite just one example, in June 1863 the Eckfords of Brooklyn invited the Athletics to their city for a full day's festivities, which neatly illustrate both the wartime context of the game and also its competitive and social aspects. The events began with a morning tour of the Continental Iron Works and the Navy Yard, where the guests viewed the construction, servicing, and repair of iron clad ships and other vessels. The men then journeyed to the Union grounds, where they devoured a "sumptuous repast." Next came the rain-shortened six inning contest, won by the Eckfords, 10–5, before a crowd of 3,000 that would probably have been much larger if the weather had not been so threatening. After the game "the victors and vanquished partook of a collation, gotten up in Eckford style, and several convivial hours were spent in discussing the savory dishes which the board afforded, and in 'ball-talk.'" The shadow of war did hang heavy over these games, but it did not spoil the sport or its accompanying socializing.

The first invasion of Philadelphia players into the New York City vicinity took place in June 1862, as a select nine of men from the Athletic, Olympic, and Adriatic clubs competed before about 15,000 spectators in a series of games against teams from Newark,

New Jersey, New York City, and Brooklyn. Although the visitors were able to win only one match (against Manhattan men at Hoboken), their tour was a resounding success. *Wilkes' Spirit* reported that "the result of their arrival has been quite an awakening of the old *furore* for the game that marked the years 1857–58 and 9 in this locality, and as far as Philadelphia is concerned, these series of games, and the triumph the Philadelphia Nine achieved at Hoboken, has done more to advance the interest and popularity of the game in that city than five ordinary season's play would have done." The *Clipper* concurred, adding that the athletes' trip "will be the means of giving an immense impetus to the game in Philadelphia, where it is rapidly taking the place of cricket." In July select nines from Brooklyn followed by the Mutuals of New York and the Eckfords of Brooklyn returned the visit later in the summer and fall, generating excitement in their contests with the local Olympics, Adriatics, Athletics, and Keystones.

The sporting exchanges between the men from Newark, Manhattan, Brooklyn, and Philadelphia continued for the duration of the war. In June 1863, as Lee's army invaded Pennsylvania and threatened an attack on the City of Brotherly Love, the home town Athletics traveled north and won two out of six games against tough competition. *Harper's Weekly* employed the war analogy in a brief commentary: "While Pennsylvania is invaded, Pennsylvania invades. While the balls of the rebels are base, it is with base-balls that the sons of the Keystone State advance upon New York. Still there is a difference. It is play that the latter come for; it is in deadly earnest that the rebels ride." That popular periodical quoted from an Athletics club announcement that explained that its trip was not undertaken "in a spirit of bravado, but rather with a view to acquire all the new points of the game—to reawaken interest in Base-Ball, and to renew associations which they have found most delightful— the good fellowship, the manliness, and the hearty hospitality of the players in and around New York having long since passed into a proverb." *Harper's Weekly* concluded by linking the sport to the military cause: "The Base-Ball Club has this great value at the present moment, that it is the 'school of the soldier' in vigor, endurance, and agility."

Highlights of the summer season of 1864 included visits by the Resolutes and Atlantics (both of Brooklyn) to the City of Brotherly Love. These intercity battles would have stirred even more public excitement, had it not been for a recent renewed Confederate attack on Pennsylvania. As the Clipper explained, the Brooklyn ball players "timed their visit at a period when the citizens were absorbed in the important subject of resisting the rebel invasion of the States, and this and the preparations to respond to the Governor's call for 30,000 militia, materially interfered with the sensation their visit would otherwise have created." It added: "Another drawback was the fact that the gallant members of the Philadelphia base ball clubs being prompt on all occasions to respond to the call of duty, were unable to aid their respective clubs with their services, and hence most of the Philadelphia clubs were unable to present their strength."

But despite the distractions of the war, these feature events did attract thousands of spectators. In general the good feeling and convivial hospitality of the preceding seasons prevailed during these matches. Philadelphia sportsmen eagerly anticipated the arrival of the celebrated Atlantics, but the results could not have pleased home town rooters, as their guests completed a four day, four game sweep over the Camden, Keystone, Olympic, and Athletic clubs. The climax of that tour was a 43–16 thrashing of the Athletics in front of a large crowd estimated at between two and three thousand spectators, including "a fair proportion of ladies." The Atlantics routed the Athletics's premier pitcher, Dick McBride, who was allowed a three-day furlough from the Union Army to face the Brooklyn team. Despite their defeat the Athletics still acquitted themselves respectably compared to the other local nines, whom the visitors trounced by scores of 64–10, 65–10, and 58–11. The *Philadelphia Inquirer* applauded the members of the Athletics, Keystones, and Olympics for entertaining their visitors and praised the character of the Atlantics. Its reporter noted: "They have made a good impression here, and go away, leaving a good name behind them."

By August it was clear that three years of intercity competition had considerably raised the level of play of the Philadelphians.

The *Clipper* was impressed by their progress in "a practical knowledge of the game," and especially that the City of Brotherly Love could "export players to fill up the ranks of some of our best clubs." The Eurekas of Newark and the Eckfords of Brooklyn each recruited Philadelphians, and the year before the Atlantics had lured away Tom Pratt from the Athletics. The *Clipper* predicted that "before the expiration of the present season we shall no doubt see matches played in which the Philadelphians for the first time will 'put in an appearance' as able contestants in the series of championship games now in progress in this vicinity."

While intercity tours spurred interest in baseball throughout the mid-Atlantic region during the war, some members of the ball playing fraternity pondered what they could contribute to the cause of the Union. Overall, while sportsmen and journalists made some effort to raise funds for wartime charities, the results were mixed at best. As early as December 1861, the annual convention of the NABBP debated a resolution that would have distributed surplus funds of the association to each volunteer in the army. But after extensive discussion the resolution was tabled because of the limited amount of money available, and also because the delegates could not agree on whether to dispense the aid to the soldiers or to the families of those "who have lost their lives in defence of their country." But although the *Clipper* suggested a "grand entertainment or ball" be scheduled that winter to raise funds for assistance to the soldiers and their families, no action seems to have been taken.

The following year the Continental Base Ball Club of Brooklyn offered a silver ball as a trophy to be awarded to the winner of a series of matches between that city's crack clubs, the Atlantics and Eckfords, with a ten cent admission charge at the recently opened Union grounds, the net proceeds to be donated to the Sanitary Commission of Brooklyn for the benefit of sick and wounded soldiers. The Eckfords won the first contest on July 11, 20–14, in front of about four thousand spectators. According to *Wilkes' Spirit*, the reputation of the clubs and "the truly philanthropic object of the pastime" attracted the crowd, which included many of the "fair sex" who added materially to the "gala-day appearance of the scene."

The Atlantics avenged their defeat on July 21 with a 39–5 rout of the Eckfords before between five and six thousand fans. About ten thousand people witnessed the deciding game on September 18, a low scoring and exciting encounter won by the Eckfords, 8–3. By their victory the Eckfords claimed not only the silver ball trophy but also the title of champions for 1862. The series demonstrated the continuing popularity of baseball in Brooklyn and throughout the New York City region. However, many of the spectators chose to evade both the admission fee and the charitable contribution by sitting on the surrounding embankments outside of the enclosure on the Union grounds.

As the wartime crisis deepened and as Union casualties mounted in 1864 the ball playing fraternity renewed its efforts to raise funds for the aid of wounded soldiers and the families of those who had lost their lives in battle. The results were rather meager. In May in Philadelphia two thousand people assembled on the Olympic club's ground on Jefferson and Twenty-fifth streets to witness an all-star game between picked nines representing the states of Pennsylvania and New Jersey. The proceeds were dedicated to the U.S. Sanitary Commission in support of the great Sanitary Fair held in that city that spring. The Jerseymen won the contest, 18–10, played under threatening weather. The *Philadelphia Inquirer* noted that "the grounds presented quite a picturesque appearance, the foliage of the trees, the bright green of the field, the various colored costumes of the ball players, together with the numerous crowd of spectators encircling the ball field, outside of which were a row of carriages, making up a *tout ensemble* of the most attractive character." The event did earn $500 for the Sanitary Fair, but unfortunately rain washed out the rest of the matches that were scheduled that week to benefit that charity.

That year the *Brooklyn Daily Eagle* hoped that the owners of that city's new Capitoline Ball Grounds would follow through on their plan to schedule a series of special matches, "half of the proceeds of which are to be given to societies connected with the Brooklyn Regiments serving in the Union army, the object being to aid the needy families of the deceased soldiers of these regiments."

But that newspaper added tellingly: "As yet our ball players have not done anything to benefit the distressed families of our soldiers, we mean, of course, as a body, and it is about time they responded to the call, and we hope they will do it as eagerly and as nobly as they have tendering their personal service in the field." In the end it seems that while many ball players enlisted and made great battlefield sacrifices, some dying of disease or wounds, those who remained on the home front made only a modest contribution to lessening the suffering of their brethren and their relatives.

While baseball clubs kept the sport alive during the nation's ordeal, the NABBP struggled to survive and to govern the game's growth. The annual December conventions in New York City experienced a sharp drop in attendance as many clubs disbanded and others did not send delegates. Local clubs from Manhattan and Brooklyn dominated these meetings, which accomplished little during the first two years of the conflict. Only thirty-four organizations were represented each year in 1861 and 1862. In 1861 the *Clipper* reported that the association's president "congratulated the fraternity on the fact of our National game having passed the trying ordeal in a manner that at once indicated the firm foothold it had attained in popular favor." *Wilkes' Spirit* was impressed with the spirit of enthusiasm in the gathering and predicted that baseball was destined to retain "its present proud and enviable position at the head of the column of American Out-Door Sports." Significantly, in 1862 the association recognized the growing excitement for baseball in Philadelphia (and the attendance of two clubs from that city) by electing Colonel Thomas Fitzgerald, president of the Athletics, as the new president of the NABBP.

In 1863 and 1864 the conventions addressed a series of major issues, acting on important rule changes and on the eligibility of players to compete in recognized interclub matches. These sessions demonstrated the continuing vitality of baseball in the New York City region and suggested the spirit of experimentation and the fluidity in rules that characterized early American baseball. The twenty-eight clubs that attended the 1863 meeting approved changes in pitching regulations that were designed to shift the balance of play toward batting and fielding. The primitive style of under-hand slow pitching prevalent in the 1850s had given the advantage to the batter, but during the early 1860s the hurlers became more expert in swift and often wild deliveries. Spectators had become impatient with the erratic pitching and the habit of some hurlers who intentionally prolonged games to avoid defeat by throwing bad balls until it became too dark to permit play to continue.

The NABBP acted to "transfer the interest of the game from the pitcher to the fielders" with new regulations that confined the pitcher to a small space, forced him to deliver "fair balls" to the batter, and required him to release the ball with both feet on the ground. Each batsman was expected to indicate his preference for the height of pitches thrown to him over home plate. Thus the definition of a "fair ball" varied with each batsman. The umpire already had the authority to call strikes on a batter who refused to swing at good pitches, but now the new rule empowered the official to award first base to the batter after three called balls. In a season preview article in May 1864 the *Clipper* expected that "a strict adherence to these rules must perforce result in there being less speed in pitching, the making of accuracy of aim the great desideratum in effective play, and the transfer of the interest of a match from the pitcher to the basemen and outfielders." That journal added: "Of course we must expect to see a large increase in scoring, the probability being that the average runs of a match will be increased from twenty to thirty in a majority of games played; but inasmuch as finer displays of fielding must necessarily ensue from these new rules, and far more enjoyable games, this increase in the scores is of no importance whatever." But of course everything depended on the judgment of umpires, and especially their willingness to enforce these new regulations.

In 1864 delegates from about thirty clubs reviewed two issues which had occupied previous meetings of the NABBP: the fly rule and eligibility of players to compete in matches. The fly rule mandated that if a batsman hit a ball in the air, a fielder had to catch the ball before it struck the ground to record an out. Opponents of this regulation argued that it would "exclude all first class catches on the bound" and also that it would lengthen games. Proponents argued that the more skillful players preferred the fly rule. After being narrowly defeated in 1863, the fly rule passed in 1864 by a vote of 32–19, with seventeen clubs in favor and eleven opposed (several clubs had more than one delegate who was eligible to vote). Like the changes of 1863, the fly rule was implemented to encourage better fielding, but of course it also gave the offense added advantage. The other significant ruling of the meeting prohibited a member of an NABBP club from participating in a match if he belonged to more than one club, no matter whether the other organization was enrolled in the NABBP or not. This regulation was also drafted to exclude members of junior clubs from playing in senior club matches.

After the NABBP excluded junior clubs in 1858, young players under the age of twenty-one from Brooklyn, Manhattan, and neighboring areas founded their own "national" organization— the National Association of Junior Base Ball Players (NAJBBP). Launched in 1860, this body met several times over the next few years, adopting the rules of the senior association and regulating its membership and championship matches. In 1861 *Wilkes' Spirit* applauded its mission and activities, calling the junior nines the "true nursery and cradle of baseball." It cited the youngsters' "enthusiasm and ardor" and the junior clubs' record of graduating their "crack players" into the ranks of the seniors. It also explained that "when the senior clubs grow slim, caused by resignation and the calls of business, the junior boys fill up their gaps, enabling them to present a full and an effective front." As noted above, this practice caused problems for the NABBP when young men competed for both junior and senior nines. Older men sometimes also appeared in junior matches, despite the prohibition of this practice by the NAJBBP in 1860. A reorganized version of the NAJBBP appeared in the summer of 1864, as junior baseball thrived in the New York City metropolitan region. In November *Wilkes' Spirit* commented favorably on youth baseball, reporting that there were at least fifty-eight regularly organized junior clubs in the metropolis and its vicinity.

During the trying times of war sporting weekly periodicals and a few daily newspapers contributed mightily to sustaining the growth of the new national pastime. Through reporting news of clubs, major and minor matches, intercity tours, and games in army camps, the *Clipper, Wilkes' Spirit*, the *Brooklyn Daily Eagle*, and other publications kept the new sport in the public eye as they distracted people's attention for a few moments from the horrific accounts of carnage on the battefields. Perhaps two of the most significant contributions made by such editors and sportswriters as Frank Queen of the *Clipper* and Henry Chadwick of several papers came in their campaigns to promote better behavior and relations among players and clubs and also to develop a system of records and statistical analysis for the game. In 1864 the *Brooklyn Daily Eagle* (probably Chadwick) proclaimed the periodical's purpose and its policy of impartiality: "One of our main objects in view is to advance the game in popularity and to make it as much of a national game of ball in this country as Cricket in England. We know no one club from another in reporting their doings, and shall continue to observe the same impartiality as long as we report the game." The writer then hinted at unpleasant prior treatment of reporters by certain clubs, and warned: "if every journal that makes base ball a specialty were to confine their notices to merely giving the scores, or were they to ignore the game altogether, it would not be the papers that would suffer, but base ball. It is the press that has made the game what it is, and it is to the aid of the press that base ball players should look to enable them to make it a permanent institution of the land." A few months later that paper prefaced an account of a bitter attack on one of its reporters by stating that its object was "to promote kindly feelings between the clubs of the city, and to benefit base ball as a national game as much as we possibly could, and in our endeavors to do this we have known no one club above another, nor have we favored one more than another, having treated all with equal consideration, wealthy and influential and poor and obscure alike."

Henry Chadwick, renown late in his life as the "Father of Baseball," pioneered the keeping of baseball records through his collection of data and his development of box and line scores, tabular standings, the annual baseball guide, and batting averages and several other forms of statistics. As historian Jules Tygiel has observed,

Chadwick was not the inventor of baseball, but he did create the game's "historical essence." Although Chadwick began his career as a cricket reporter, not long after he became interested in baseball he began experimenting with methods of giving detailed reports of leading matches. While he produced his first recorded baseball box score in 1859, it was during the war years that he intensified his efforts at accurate record keeping and scientific statistical analysis of the sport. An example of his passion for numbers appears in the *Brooklyn Daily Eagle* on October 31, 1863, when he was absorbed with the tedious task of gathering all of the data for that season to compute the year's averages for players. He wrote: "The making out of these averages is an exceedingly difficult and intricate task, but as it is a subject deeply interesting to every ball player, we have undertaken it every season, being the first to inaugurate the plan. Had every club a regularly appointed scorer and one fully competent to take down a record of the game in such a manner that a correct estimate of the season's play of every member could be obtained from the score book, each Secretary of a club could readily make up the club averages; but the reverse is the case, for not only are scorers as a general thing in the habit of recording the game in the old-fashioned and incorrect style, but not one out of every five knows how to put down the particulars as they ought to be recorded."

Intercity tours, benefit matches, conventions, and sports-writers all helped early baseball sustain itself during the Civil War. But the greatest proof of the vitality of the new national pastime appeared in the clubs founded and the games played by schoolboys, college students, and adult men from a variety of social classes, nationalities, and races. Girls and women also were showing interest, primarily as spectators, and by 1865 a few of them were active participants. By the end of the war baseball had already exhibited some growing pains, as championship competition, commercialism, and professionalism raised some troubling issues about the national pastime. Major matches between rival clubs also demonstrated some of the stresses and strains of northern urban society as the nation passed through its most critical ordeal.

4

Players and Clubs

I n 1862 Albert G. Spalding's mother sent her twelve year-old son to Rockford, Illinois, to board with his aunt and attend public school. Young Spalding was a shy, homesick, and lonesome country boy from a small village who found consolation and an escape from his depression through baseball. As he watched other boys playing ball on the town commons he desperately wanted to join in the fun and action, but he could not summon up the nerve to assert himself. Fortunately, he recalled later, "special Providence" intervened when a youth smacked a long ball "straight as an arrow" in his direction as he sat behind the center fielder. He remembered: "Impulsively I sprang to my feet, reached out for it with my right hand, held it for a moment and then threw it home on an air line to the catcher." That feat impressed his peers enough to earn him an invitation to join in their regular games. Before long he was one of the first to be chosen when sides were selected. Three years later he was pitching for a local Rockford adult club, which launched him on a career marked by fame and fortune as a star hurler, manager, club president, and sporting goods magnate in the world of professional baseball.

1862 turned out to be the last year of competition for a baseball superstar who created a sensation with a novel style of swift underhand pitching. Born in New York City in 1841, Jim Creighton moved with his family to Brooklyn and made a name for himself with a few junior teams before the Excelsiors recruited him in 1860, probably by offering him some compensation. More than six feet tall, with long arms and a muscular build, he dominated opponents with his low, swift, rising and spinning fastballs. He was also a star cricketer—a skilled batsman and a first-class bowler for the St. George Cricket Club of New York. Friendly and multi-talented, he was much admired within the ball playing fraternity. After his untimely death in 1862 at the age of twenty-one the *Brooklyn Daily Eagle* described him as "warm in his attachments, gifted with a large measure of humor, an enthusiastic and practical musician, and a most agreeable conversationalist."

Creighton's talent and the tragic (and controversial) circumstances of his death transformed him into baseball's first legendary character. In later years a myth circulated that he had ruptured his bladder after hitting a home run in a game against the Union club on October 14, and then suffered from the effects of this injury for a few days before he expired on October 18. This story is based in part on an obituary published in the *Brooklyn Daily Eagle*, and also on testimony of teammates who remembered that Creighton told them that he thought that he had snapped his belt as he swung his bat during the game against the Union nine. However, a report in the *Clipper* stated that his death was caused by "internal injuries, resulting from a severe strain he received while batting a ball" in his last cricket match, when he bowled for the St. George eleven against the Willow club on October 9. Newspaper accounts of that match praise Creighton's batting and bowling that day, but make no mention of any injury. Furthermore, in December 1864 Dr. Joseph Jones, an officer of the Excelsior club, told the delegates to the annual NABBP convention that Creighton's injury had occurred in a cricket match and not a baseball game. Researcher Tom Shieber has concluded that Creighton died of a strangulated intestine. It is possible and perhaps even likely that Creighton did first injure himself in the cricket match against the Willow club on October 9, because he did not pitch in the first five innings of the baseball game against the Union. The story and box score of that game indicate that he did pitch the sixth (and final inning) and had four doubles, but no home runs. In all probability he hurt himself in the cricket match on October 9, aggravated that injury in the baseball game on October 14, and died from intestinal complications four days later. He was buried in Brooklyn's Greenwood Cemetery, his fame honored with a monument that featured a granite bat and ball. Within a few years teams visiting New York City made pilgrimages to his grave.

During the war years two brothers, William Henry (Harry) and George Wright, perfected their baseball skills and took the first steps toward their ultimate enshrinement at Cooperstown in the Hall of Fame. Harry Wright was born in Sheffield, England in 1835. As a toddler he traveled with his parents to New York City in 1836, and a few years later his father Samuel became the professional for the St. George Cricket Club of Manhattan. Young Harry attended grade school in New York and then was employed by a jewelry manufacturer. But his true love was athletics; as a young man during the 1850s he excelled as a professional bowler for the Dragon Slayers of St. George. At that time he also took up the game of baseball, playing with the Knickerbockers before switching to the more talented Gothams. After the Civil War he accepted a position as a professional cricket player for the Union Cricket Club of Cincinnati, but within a few years he switched his allegiance to baseball. Captain, pitcher, and then center fielder for the new Cincinnati Red Stockings Base Ball Club, in 1869 he organized, managed, and starred for the nation's first fully professional baseball team. During the 1870s he was a central figure in the creation of both the National Association of Professional Base Ball Players and the National League. He was elected to the Hall of Fame in 1953.

Harry Wright's younger brother George was born in Yonkers, New York in 1847. He was a sportsman who had a distinguished athletic career as a cricketer, baseball player, sporting goods merchant, and pioneer of American golf. As a boy and young man during the 1860s he starred in cricket for the St. George club and for several baseball nines in Manhattan and Philadelphia. In 1869–70 he gained fame as the hard-hitting shortstop of the Red Stockings. He was a premier performer in both the National Association and the National League until his retirement in 1882. After his playing days ended he concentrated his energies on his sporting goods business. In the 1890s he was one of the first to introduce the Scottish game of golf in the Boston area. He was inducted into the Hall of Fame in 1937.

Al Reach never made it into the Hall of Fame, but his career as a baseball player and his success as a sporting goods manufacturer during the late 1800s earned him a reputation as one of the most prominent sportsmen of his era. Born in London, England in 1840, he grew up in Brooklyn. Like the Wright brothers, as a boy he played both cricket and baseball, but turned to the latter sport to find fame and fortune. A star with the Eckfords during the war years, he accepted an offer of $25 as "expense money" to join the Athletics of Philadelphia in 1865. Some historians believe that compensation (roughly equal to a few weeks' wages for an average worker) made him the first paid professional in baseball, while others credit that distinction to Creighton. In any case Reach played twelve seasons for the Athletics as a left-handed second baseman.

Octavius V. Catto was an African American who lived a short but energetic life as a star baseball player, teacher, and civil rights advocate. Born in 1839 in Charleston, South Carolina, he was the son of a Presbyterian minister who brought his family to Philadelphia in 1844. A graduate of that town's Institute for Colored Youth, Catto later served there as a teacher and principal. During the war he campaigned for Lincoln's re-election in 1864 in Virginia. He also enlisted in a "colored" local militia in Philadelphia. After he war he served as Inspector General to the Fifth Brigade of the Pennsylvania National Guard. Initially a cricket player during his high school years, he apparently switched to baseball during the war. During the postwar period Catto joined the Pennsylvania Equal Rights League, worked for the desegregation of Philadelphia street-cars and became a confirmed Republican dedicated to gaining the right to vote for all African-Americans. Admitted to the city's prestigious Franklin Institute, he had just launched himself into national prominence when an assassin's bullet cut short his life in October 1871. His untimely passing was mourned by both races and his funeral was one of the largest ever held for a black man in Philadelphia. His death deprived the city of a black sports hero and civil rights leader and severely damaged the cause of racial equality in the City of Brotherly Love.

Spalding, Creighton, the Wright brothers, Reach, and Catto were only six of the thousands of people who enjoyed playing or watching baseball during the civil war era and who ensured that the game would thrive after the return of peace. Native and foreigner, young and old, white and black, male and female, craftsman and clerk, merchant and manager, affluent and humble, all took part in the action. In most if not all cities and towns baseball players ranged from young boys to men well into middle age. Many youngsters from a wide range of social classes had long enjoyed premodern versions of the game, and when the Knickerbocker rules became popular they embraced the new form with great excitement. In October 1865 the *Newark Daily Advertiser* reported a "Carnival of Base Ball" in that New Jersey city and suggested that "there is not an urchin in Newark" who did not belong to a club that emulated the senior nines. It explained: "In that little republic of base ball, the child of wealth is seen playing with the youthful ragamuffins from some neighboring alley, and the magic ball passes swiftly from the pretty hand of the patrician boy to the soiled fist of the little plebian. When, indeed, we see the general interest manifested among all classes in this manly and healthful sport, not only in our own city but throughout the country, we must acknowledge that it is rightfully called the National Game of America."

The sport was also embraced by many adults in their twenties and thirties, and it was not uncommon to see active participants in their forties and even fifties. The veterans of Newark's Knickerbocker Base Ball Club continued to play the old style of ball that they enjoyed forty years earlier, while the hometown Eurekas defeated the New York Empires in "an exhibition by the supernumerary and superannuated of both organizations."

At the grass-roots level of early American baseball many boys honed their skills on open lots, streets, and fields in cities, towns, and villages, while young and older men engaged in factory, shop, and office contests. Many enthusiasts of early forms of "folkball" ignored local ordinances banning sports on the Sabbath. Sunday sports were popular for those who had little or no other leisure time, but factory workers, shop artisans, and white-collar employees sometimes played pickup games on weekdays, either during lunch breaks or after work. In 1860 the *Newark Daily Advertiser* remarked: "The streets in the vicinity of our factories are now full at noon and evening of apprentices and others engaged in the simpler games of ball, thus counteracting the injurious effects of the sedentary pursuits in which some of them are engaged." Firemen, pressmen, compositors, news agents, postal employees, harness makers, minstrel troops, engravers, Treasury Department plate printers, jewelers, sawyers, iron workers, grocers, hat finishers, plumbers, and many other groups challenged rivals to friendly tests of skill on the diamond. In 1864 New York City's Central Park commissioners, who were reluctant to allow anyone to use the new baseball grounds, received "some twenty or thirty applications from the employees of several manufacturing establishments."

When workers challenged their counterparts in other businesses in a game of ball, the matches were usually contested in a spirit of friendliness. While some employers were skeptical about their workers playing baseball, many others endorsed the ball playing craze that was sweeping America. Sometimes these events were comical affairs, as when overweight saloon keepers of rival Newark wards faced each other, or when "muffin matches" between inept players were arranged to provide fun for competitors and spectators. But there were some exceptional encounters for championship honors that became quite serious affairs. Matters became more intense when company nines played for the championship of their trade, especially when there were suspicions that one side had recruited outsiders to gain an advantage.

Games between employees of newspapers were popular and usually featured "good feeling manifested by the contesting nines towards each other, all the ill natured rivalry of the opposing journals being confined to the editorial department." During this period Thanksgiving Day was recognized as the closing date for the baseball season. In November 1863 *Wilkes' Spirit* reported that it was a "festive occasion for those of the 'typos' who are at all affected with

71

base ball on the brain." It explained that compositors of various metropolitan journals planned contests for that holiday, including one match between two nines from Brooklyn's *Union* and *Eagle* newspapers. It highlighted a political overtone to that encounter when it noted: "The 'Repubs' of the former boldly challenged the 'Cops' [Democratic Copperheads] of the latter."

As baseball evolved during the 1860s it became more organized, specialized, and scientific. Professionalism, commercialism, and scientific play eventually subordinated the element of fun in favor of the spirit of work. The game took on more of the trappings of big business and both mirrored and reinforced many of the tendencies of modern American life. Yet the amateur players of the Civil War era competed more for the love of play and retained more of the premodern ways of early American "folk-ball." They found temporary refuge from their sober responsibilities as husbands, fathers, providers, and workers on baseball fields.

America's first baseball clubs were private associations. Political, religious, charitable, educational, and cultural societies were popular in colonial and Revolutionary America, and they multiplied during the rapid urbanization of the 1800s. As the pressures of life in the cities intensified, and as social diversity and tensions mounted, city people sought reaffirmation of their identities as well as recreation and relaxation in sports clubs. These organizations provided social interaction, exercise for health, and various levels of competition for all grades of athletes. They permitted people who shared common values to play together, and these clubs' proliferation during the Civil War era marked a critical stage in the development of modern American sports. These clubs embodied and fostered the early bureaucratization of athletics in the United States.

A baseball club was established every time a few enthusiasts succeeded in recruiting enough players who were willing to attend meetings, appear on practice days, and support all club activities. Age was a decisive factor in choosing club members. Skill level, physical maturity, and cultural norms all dictated that men and boys should not play or socialize together. Baseball clubs had three age categories: boys (sixteen and under), juniors (young men under twenty-one), and seniors. There were many exceptions to these limits, of course, as talented boys sometimes played with older adolescents, while skilled juniors competed with adults. In some cases it is difficult to classify an entire team. The *Clipper* reported in 1861 that two Brooklyn clubs competing for the junior championship were "not composed of boys, but of young men, many of whom [were] older than the younger members of the senior organizations."

As public opinion during the 1850s shifted toward a more favorable attitude toward physical education and sport for America's youth, many schools, academies, and colleges sanctioned student-sponsored baseball clubs. Baseball prospered on several college campuses in the North during the Civil War era, despite the distractions of the emergency and the loss of some students who chose to enlist in the Union or Confederate armies. Some who remained on college campuses during the fighting were too young to serve, while others wished to finish their studies before volunteering or simply chose to avoid the danger of battle.

The rage for the game at Williams, Amherst, Harvard, Princeton, and other institutions originated in the late 1850s, as undergraduates created the clubs and varsity teams that pioneered modern intercollegiate athletics. During that decade college sports originated as part of a general student reaction against the strict discipline and rigid curriculum imposed by administrations. The young men responded by founding literary and debating societies, fraternities, magazines, and political, musical, and religious clubs. Those who were more physically inclined naturally turned to athletic clubs, with rowing leading the way. Harvard and Yale inaugurated intercollegiate athletics in the United States with a crew race in August 1852.

Seven years later baseball teams from Amherst and Williams played a match by the "Massachusetts" rules, with Amherst easily winning the first intercollegiate baseball game, 73–33, at Pittsfield, Massachusetts in early July 1859. The *Pittsfield Sun* reported that only a few students from Amherst attended because its administration had not granted its undergraduates a holiday, "but from Williams, where the Faculty *were more liberal*, nearly all the students were in attendance, and some of them were accompanied by ladies from Williamstown." After the contest the Pittsfield Base Ball club hosted a dinner for the college teams. The next day Amherst completed a sweep of its weekend competition with Williams by winning a match game at chess.

The premier college baseball team of the war years represented Princeton, then known as the College of New Jersey. During the fall of 1857 a few members of the freshman class organized the Nassau Baseball Club, but they were upstaged the following autumn by a group of newcomers from Brooklyn. L. W. Mudge, H. S. Butler, and H. L. Sampson of the class of 1862 had played for the Star Club of their native city—the hotbed of baseball fever in the nation in the late 1850s. Before long they had taken charge of the game in Princeton, and by 1860 they and other classmates had appropriated their predecessors' name for their nine—the Nassau Baseball Club. They competed in intramural games and also matches against teams from the nearby Seminary. Their first excursion off campus occurred in October of 1860, when the Faculty gave the players permission to travel to Orange, New Jersey to compete against a team composed mostly of Princeton alumni.

The reputation of the Nassau nine grew two years later, when the Princetonians claimed the championship of New Jersey with two victories over the Stars of New Brunswick. After the first win in late September in Princeton the club officers had some difficulty extracting permission from the college's president (Dr. John Maclean) to play a road game on a Saturday afternoon. But after he relented the young men boarded a train to New Brunswick on October 11. After their arrival their hosts entertained them with a game of billiards and a tour of the "rustic village." Highlights of the excursion by the ball players were "a number of churches and houses, plenty of Jersey mud, college, seminary, and a few pretty girls with skirts fastened (enchantingly) up to avoid the wet." After the Nassau triumph the defeated Stars entertained their guests with a fine supper. The *Nassau Literary Magazine* proudly concluded its report on this match by announcing: "We have a fine Base Ball Club in College; it is a magnificent game in itself, and while other colleges have numerous other diversions, it is the only practicable manly sport at Princeton."

10. Princeton Class of 1861: Baseball Nine. During the Civil War the Nassau Baseball Club of the College of New Jersey (later renamed Princeton) adopted the rules of the New York game, largely because of the influence of students from Brooklyn. Used with permission of Princeton University Library, University Archives. Department of Rare Books and Special Collections.

Encouraged by their victories over the former champions of New Jersey, over the next two years the Nassaus challenged several of the most prominent clubs of Philadelphia, Newark, New York, and Brooklyn. In May of 1863 a trip to Philadelphia produced a defeat by the Athletics but a win over the Olympics. In late September the Princetonians gained revenge against the Athletics with a 29–13 victory, played on a hilly field, which, according to a Philadelphia newspaper, "No one but a topographical engineer could describe." The *Philadelphia Inquirer* reported that the Saturday of the game was "a gala day in the college world of Princeton," and the

11. Princeton Baseball Nine, 1863–64. During these years the Nassau nine fielded one of the strongest teams in New Jersey and inaugurated a series with Williams College. Used with permission of Princeton University Library, University Archives. Department of Rare Books and Special Collections.

undergraduates were "most distressingly attacked by that very prevalent disease, in this mild foretaste of an Indian summer weather— *Baseball on the brain.*" Even more impressive was a vacation week trip to Brooklyn in October, when the Nassau nine defeated the Resolutes, Excelsiors, and Stars, losing only to the mighty Atlantics. The visit turned out to be a satisfying homecoming for many of the students who were natives of Brooklyn. Their performance earned high praise from the *Clipper*, whose reporter noted: "They have done what no other club has done that has ever visited the Metropolis

12. Princeton Baseball Nine, 1865–1866. Princeton's ball players continued to compete against New Jersey and collegiate teams during the postwar period. Used with permission of Princeton University Library, University Archives. Department of Rare Books and Special Collections.

before, viz: won three out of four games with Brooklyn Clubs." After the school year ended in June of 1864 the Nassau club toured the greater New York City metropolitan region in early July, scoring victories over the Mutuals of New York and the Stars of Brooklyn, but losing to the Atlantics and the Eurekas of Newark.

1864 also witnessed the debut of the Nassau nine in intercollegiate competition. Back in the fall of 1860 Captain Mudge had written to undergraduates of Yale, Columbia, and Rutgers, challenging them to a baseball match, but his correspondents had replied that those institutions had no regular teams, and were still playing by the older townball rules. In September 1863 the *Nassau Literary Magazine* reported that "the Nassau B.B.C. has thrown down the gauntlet before all the Colleges in the country, challenging them to play a game of base ball during vacation." The day finally arrived in late November of 1864 when a group of Williams students, resplendent in bright uniforms, lost to their hosts, who played in plain clothes. According to the *Nassau Literary Magazine*, the 27–16 win by the Nassaus was especially bitter for the visitors, as "the Williams men felt disgusted because they were beaten by a crowd of 'countries' in shirt sleeves." But the Williams team gained a measure of revenge the following June, when they won the rematch at Williamstown, 30–17.

Harvard students also joined in the mania for baseball during the Civil War era. In 1858 thirty-five undergraduates joined several graduates and others to form the Lawrence Base Ball Club in Cambridge. They adopted the New York rules and played intrasquad games and regular contests against a nine of law students. Although that club became inactive after the outbreak of hostilities in 1861, the following year a group of freshmen from Phillips Exeter Academy organized the '66 Baseball Club. Frank Wright remembered that he and a few of his fellow Harvard undergraduates got the idea to start a baseball team during a Latin recitation class, during which they passed a note around the room asking for volunteers to attend an organizational meeting. At that gathering a majority initially wanted to play by the rules of the Massachusetts game, but Wright recalled that "a few of us who hailed from New York state carried the meeting in favor of the new game, then called the 'Brooklyn' game." Wright and fellow student George Flagg then selected a uniform with a crimson "H" on the shirt, but when a Boston seamstress persuaded them to use a magenta "H" they switched to the color that all Harvard athletic teams later adopted. Wright, Flagg, and a few others gained permission from the Cambridge city government to lay out a diamond on the town's common for practice games played by Harvard undergraduates and members of other Boston clubs. A highlight of the 1863 season was a victory by a Harvard team over the Brown University class of '65 at Providence, Rhode

Abercrombie   Smith   Flagg, *Capt.*   Ames   Hunnewell

Nelson   Wright   Parker   Banker

13. Harvard Baseball Nine, 1866. Harvard's class of 1866 founded the college's baseball club in 1862, adopting the rules of the New York game. Its initial success against local teams and New England colleges laid the foundation for Harvard's rise to prominence as the leading college club during the late 1860s. Used with permission of the New York Public Library. General Research Division, Astor, Lenox and Tilden Foundations.

Island. The following spring the team gained permission from the faculty to lay out a field on the "Delta" on the college campus.

The pace of baseball activity quickened at Harvard in the summer and fall of 1864, when its first nine of the sophomore class easily defeated a team from Bowdoin College in Maine but suffered a surprising setback to the sophomores of Williams in a match played in late July at a rowing regatta at Worcester, Massachusetts. Harvard had been the favorite because of its victories over Brown and Bowdoin, with its only loss coming at the hands of the crack Lowell club of Boston. But the men from Williams prevailed 12–9, even though (according to the *Clipper*) "they had the biennial examination, the bugbear of students, on their hands," and they had to pick a first

J. D'W. Lovett   W. H. Alline   W. B. Joslin R. C. Watson   A. Crosby
        S. Adams   G. S. Miller (Capt.)   G. B. Wilder   F. H. Sumner

LOWELL BASEBALL NINE, 1865

14. Lowell Baseball Nine, 1865. This prominent Boston club was one of the first in New England to adopt the rules of the New York game. It hosted the Excelsiors of Brooklyn in 1862 and sponsored a local tournament in 1864 and 1865. Used with permission of the New York Public Library. General Research Division, Astor, Lenox and Tilden Foundations.

nine from only forty players, compared to one hundred available to Harvard. In October Flagg and Wright led a reorganization of the class nines into the Harvard University Base Ball Club, which adopted a grey uniform that featured a large "H" on the shirt. *Wilkes' Spirit* remarked approvingly that "the national game has become an established institution at Harvard; and another season, when the University nine is made up, the contests will become quite exciting." The next season brought peace to the nation and a regional title to the new University nine, as it defeated the Lowell Club of Boston 28–17 on July 15, 1865 for a silver ball trophy emblematic of the championship of New England. Four days later the Harvard men extended their winning streak with a 35–20 triumph over Williams.

In other northeastern colleges during this era many students formed class or varsity baseball teams, generally adopting the rules of the National Association of Base Ball Players. At Bowdoin in 1860 each class organized a baseball club with two nines, and although interest in the sport declined after the outbreak of war, a college team competed against Harvard in 1864. Elsewhere in New England undergraduates played baseball at Brown, Tufts, Yale, and Norwich (Vermont), while in New York (state and city) college students founded clubs at Hamilton, the Free Academy (later the City College of New York), Fordham, Columbia, and New York University. Across the Hudson in New Jersey undergraduates at Seton Hall enlisted in the baseball fraternity.

In the Midwest in the spring of 1863 John Marshall "Jack" Hinchman, one of the stars of the Brother Jonathan Base Ball Club of Detroit, joined with Emory Grant of Wisconsin to pioneer baseball at the University of Michigan at Ann Arbor. During that inaugural season he wrote to his parents that he was playing the game two or three times a week, and he asked his younger brother to send him a box of baseball equipment. By the middle of June the university had a first nine that announced a claim to contend for the state championship, but matches could not be arranged due to upcoming final examinations. The following year the war severely curtailed baseball activity throughout the state, but the University of Michigan nine remained active with intrasquad games and matches against Ann Arbor High School and the State Normal School in Ypsilanti (now Eastern Michigan University).

Although baseball surged in popularity during the late 1850s when tens of thousands of European immigrants arrived in the United States, the overwhelming majority of players were native-born. Yet before the outbreak of the war, hundreds of Irish names appeared on the rosters of major and minor clubs, especially in Brooklyn and in Newark, Jersey City, and Orange, New Jersey. During the Civil War era the Irish who excelled at the new national pastime paved the way for the next generation of their countrymen,

CHAPTER FOUR

who became the dominant ethnic group in the sport well into the twentieth century. A scattering of German and other central European newcomers joined these Irish athletes.

While African-Americans constituted only a small percentage of the total population of the centers of early American baseball, several of them enthusiastically adopted the new game. There is evidence that links their earliest participation in the sport to the issue of greater opportunity for blacks in American society. On July 4, 1859 Joshua Giddings, a white antislavery Republican Congressman, played in a game with African-Americans. In the fall of 1860 the Unknown Club and Colored Union Club of Brooklyn played a game, while two years later the *Brooklyn Daily Eagle* began an account of a local contest between the Unknowns of Weeksville and the Monitors of Brooklyn with the headline: "A New Sensation in Baseball Circles—Sambo as a Ball-Player and Dinah as an Emulator." Its reporter noticed among the spectators "a number of old and well known players, who seemed to enjoy the game more heartily than if they had been the players themselves." The contest was played in mid-October of 1862, just weeks after President Lincoln had announced his Emancipation Proclamation freeing slaves in rebel-held counties in the Confederacy. While the *Eagle* was not sympathetic to the abolitionist cause, its writer tellingly stated: "It would have done Beecher, Greeley, or any other of the luminaries of the radical wing of the Republican Party good to have been present." In the fall of 1862 The *Newark Daily Advertiser* also reported that "considerable excitement was created among the colored 'boys' of this city . . . by a base ball match between the Hamilton Club of this city and the Henson Club of Jamaica, L.I., both composed of the descendants of Ham." While there may have been no direct connection between Lincoln's Emancipation Proclamation and this flurry of baseball activity among African-Americans in the autumn of 1862, certainly their participation did raise issues of equal opportunity in the sport that would become prominent in the immediate postwar era.

Most of the pioneers of American baseball came from the white native-born upper and middle classes of professionals, business managers, petty proprietors, clerks, and skilled craftsmen. Although

82

the wealthiest urbanites preferred the more exclusive sports of horse racing or yachting, many of those who ranked just below the most affluent embraced the new pastime with great affection. For example, William Cauldwell of the Morrisania (Bronx) Unions owned the *New York Sunday Mercury*. The New York Gothams's Seamen Lichtenstein lived a true rags-to-riches life. Born into poverty in 1825 and orphaned as a young boy, he founded what became one of the largest produce houses in the United States. Lichtenstein served as the Gothams's treasurer from 1857 to 1859 and also owned and raced horses in his later years with such luminaries as William H. Vanderbilt. Although New York's Knickerbocker Base Ball club was not as exclusive or as fashionable as that city's leading athletic and social clubs, it did enroll several men who distinguished themselves in business. James Fowler Wenman, a first-nine shortstop during the 1850s, came from a prominent Irish family. During his playing days he traded in cotton, and in 1861 he organized the Board of New York Cotton Brokers; over the next several decades he prospered as president, vice president, and manager of the New York Cotton Exchange. Wenman kept up his interest in recreation by serving as a Central Park commissioner during the 1870s.

Joining these managers and professionals on the ball fields were numerous petty proprietors, office workers, and skilled craftsmen who were acquiring property and status in America's cities and towns during these years. Among these middle class players was Hampton A. Coursen of the Jersey City Hamiltons, born in Sussex County, New Jersey, in 1826. Like many players, he was a member of a volunteer fire department; he also became senior member of a wholesale liquor firm and a director of the Hudson County Bank of Jersey City and the North River Insurance Company of New York. Rochus Heinisch, an active player and umpire for the Newark Base Ball Club during the 1850s, was born in 1801 in Austria, where he learned the cutlery trade. He moved to Newark around 1834 and began a successful career as a manufacturer of patent shears and razors; he was also a member of the city council.

The extensive participation of artisans in the national pastime is noteworthy at a time when metropolitan industrialization had a major impact on many crafts. Skilled craftsmen in such fields as carpentry, blacksmithing, food preparation, and shipbuilding had sufficient income and time for leisure sports such as baseball. Workers, however, who labored under the direction of master craftsmen to produce clothing, shoes, hats, furniture, and other items found that the advent of the first machines and the new organization of manufacturing standardized and often accelerated the pace of work. They experienced deteriorating conditions, performing repetitious tasks in tight quarters with little or no break before lunch or at the end of the day. Hatters, shoemakers, trunk makers, and others in such trades sought recreation on ball fields whenever they could find the time; sometimes their bosses cooperated and even joined in the action. Given the nature of the work of compositors and pressmen and their relatively high wages, it is not surprising that many of them took up baseball. There were numerous early baseball players who lived out their lives as more humble mechanics or semiskilled or unskilled workers. These men included baseball-playing Irish laborers, hatters, policemen, and other common people who joined the sports boom of the 1850s, and who have long been forgotten.

A few females braved ridicule by joining the boys and men who created modern baseball. Women first visited ball fields as spectators, but before long some of them wanted to be players themselves. Most baseball clubs made a special effort to encourage ladies to attend their matches by providing them with tents, seats, refreshments, and other accommodations. Sportsmen believed that female spectators would enhance the respectability of their pastimes while they also restrained the behavior of males in the crowds. The sporting weeklies and daily press cooperated by urging women to patronize baseball. The *Brooklyn Daily Eagle*, for example, recommended baseball as "a rational and manly pastime, which our wives, sisters, and sweethearts can witness, and enliven us with their presence, without the fear of a word or deed that would call the blush to the cheek of the most fastidious." Frank Queen, editor of the *Clipper*, suspected that women attended sporting events primarily for social reasons, and he wanted them to exert their positive influence on troublemakers: "Let our American ladies visit the cricket grounds, the regattas, the baseball matches, and the most rough or rude among the spectators would acknowledge their magic sway. . . . When ladies are present . . . no class of our population can be found so debased as not to change their external behavior immediately, and that change is always for the better." Before the war *Porter's Spirit* remarked that contestants exerted extra energy to perform well in front of ladies and speculated about the women that "more than one of them attends the ground with the view of sharply measuring among the players the qualities of what might make a serviceable future husband." During the Civil War the sporting press continued to applaud sportsmen who welcomed women at their contests.

Females did appear in sizeable numbers at ball grounds, especially for the premier interclub, all-star, and international contests. On several occasions they showed their approbation of the new team sports as moral, wholesome recreations by presenting the participants with American flags or bouquets of flowers. In New Jersey, delegations of women frequently participated in postgame awards rituals. Newspaper descriptions of their attire suggest that most of the women who attended these matches were from the "respectable" middle and upper classes. Others came out of curiosity or because of the beauty and excitement of the play. More than a few were well acquainted with the fine points of the sport and were vociferous fans. The *Clipper* reported that among a crowd of spectators who watched a match on Boston Common in June 1858 were "ladies, who, from the waving of handkerchiefs, and peals of merry laughter, were evidently delighted with the sport." Some women apparently joined in the gambling as well—for example, at the second game of the 1858 Fashion Race Course series, when *Porter's Spirit* stated that "ladies were found exchanging little wagers among themselves."

While it is likely that a few girls and young women played baseball during the Civil War, after 1865 female participation increased significantly. In 1866 the young ladies of the newly founded Vassar College fielded several baseball "eights," including the Laurel and Abenakis clubs. In 1867 the baseball fever in Bordentown, New

Jersey "reached the female persuasion," and a heated rivalry began between the Belle Vue and Galazy clubs. At Peterboro, New York, the granddaughter of women's rights advocate Gerrit Smith was the captain of a girls' baseball club that enrolled about fifty members. She and her friends practiced out of town, "away from the gaze of the curious who would naturally crowd around such a beautiful display." Dispensing with "all the riotous petticoats and flummery," they adopted a costume "which must have carried insubordination into the ranks of the male assemblage" and played a public game before a large crowd. They wore "short blue and white tunics, reaching to the knees, straw caps, jauntily trimmed, white stockings and stout gaiter shoes." In Rockford, Illinois, a "picked nine of maidens" defeated a married ladies' club, while at Northwestern Female College at Evanston, two nines from the Diana club attracted many curious spectators. Girls' teams also appeared in Cincinnati and Lancaster, Ohio. Thus white middle-class American-born school and college girls and young ladies were the pioneers of early women's baseball. They broke down male resistance to female ball playing and at the same time blazed the trail for their sisters of all ages, nationalities, races, and classes to compete on the diamonds of America.

As boys and college students enthusiastically adopted baseball and ensured that the new pastime would have a bright future after the war, their adult counterparts received most of the attention of the public at large and the sporting press in particular. Among senior baseball players, occupation appears to have been the major factor in club formation, although wealth and ward residence (in larger cities) were also influential. While some organizations were either predominantly white- or blue-collar, many were fairly evenly mixed. All of the baseball cities had their predominant white-collar clubs of merchants, managers, lawyers, doctors, clerks, actors, and petty professionals. These included the New York Knickerbockers and Metropolitans, the Brooklyn Excelsiors, the Boston Olympics, Bay Staters, and Tri-Mountains, the Newark Knickerbocker Antiquarians, the Jersey City Hamiltons, and the Philadelphia Olympics, Athletics, and Mercantiles.

While large numbers of middle- and upper middle-class men joined these white-collar clubs, perhaps an equal or greater number of blue-collar players formed working-class clubs. Unlike the numerous factory and trade nines discussed earlier, these were formally organized associations that existed apart from any company or business connection. Brooklyn boasted two of the most powerful teams of skilled workers: the Atlantics and the Eckfords. Both had large working-class followings. Frank Pidgeon, one of the leaders of the early Eckfords, recalled that he and his teammates found in baseball an escape and diversion from their occupations, as well as physical exercise and psychological refreshment. They thrived on the excitement generated and the camaraderie; they frolicked for the fun of being young again. He remarked: "We had some merry times among ourselves; we would forget business and everything else, on Tuesday afternoons, go out into the green fields, don our ball suits, and go at it with a perfect rush. At such times, we were boys again. Such sport as this brightens a man up, and improves him, both in mind and body." Since these blue-collar clubs were not under the direct influence of factory, shop, or company owners, they were free to demonstrate independence and class consciousness, though we do not know the extent to which these teams asserted the solidarity and feelings of working men. The clubs did combine premodern and modern characteristics in their mixture of drinking and horseplay with serious, hard practice and intense competitiveness, and there were occasional instances of class identification by their supporters during match play—as, for example, when the Atlantics or the Eckfords competed against white-collar clubs.

American baseball fielded several clubs with an evenly divided blue- and white-collar membership during its amateur era. The Newark Base Ball Club, as well as that city's Adriatic and Lafayette nines, represented this type. The Newark club, founded in 1855, included a variety of skilled craftsmen, petty proprietors, clerks, and bookkeepers of moderate wealth. The Adriatics—the most affluent of Newark's baseball fraternity—were primarily jewelers, merchants, and professionals. The Lafayettes brought together men from the building and leather trades, along with some clerks and merchants. All of these examples suggest that when blue- and white-collar workers formed a baseball club, their common economic status or residence outweighed their vocational differences. In fact, even those clubs that were predominantly working-class had some white-collar members, and vice versa.

Politics or religion could also determine the membership of these early athletic associations. For example, volunteer fire companies frequently sponsored baseball clubs; some of these had close ties with political parties. The most famous example of a baseball team with a fire company connection was New York's Mutual club, which eventually became an instrument of Manhattan's notorious politician, William M. "Boss" Tweed, after the Civil War. Tammany Hall politicians founded the Mutual Base Ball Club in Manhattan in 1857, naming it after the Mutual Hook and Ladder Company #1. Most of its officers and many of its players were employed by the city in the offices of the coroner or the street commissioner, and the club also received public funds. John Wildey, its president, was the city coroner and a prominent Tammany official. Tweed himself was never a major office holder in the Mutuals, but he contributed generously to the club's finances. During the war several transplanted New Yorkers and Brooklynites worked for the Treasury Department in Washington, D.C., and played for the National and Union clubs on fenced-in grounds at the rear of the White House. After the war the Nationals challenged the Mutuals, Atlantics, Athletics, and other premier clubs for championship honors.

There is also some evidence that a few churches sponsored teams, despite the traditional Protestant coolness toward sport. The players on New York's Alpine club belonged to the Jane Street Methodist Episcopal Church, for which "religion and healthful out-of-door exercise [were] not incompatible." In 1865 a group of prominent Philadelphia clergymen formed a baseball club and appeared in public "as athletes, in true club style—belts, caps, and all."

Before a group of players could consider themselves a baseball club in good standing, they had to choose a name, ratify a constitution and bylaws, adopt a uniform, and find a suitable playing ground. The selection of a name was the simplest of these procedures. While some baseball players selected local place names, such as cities, towns, or counties, others preferred patriotic, sporting, Indian, or other titles. Considering the intense interest in nationalism during the Civil War era, it is not surprising that common names were Union, Independent, Liberty, Washington, Lafayette, Hamilton, Pioneer, Columbia, Empire, Continental, Eagle, Americus, Young America, and National. Within the sporting category, Olympic, Athletic, and Exercise were popular. Other favorites were Excelsior, Active, Alert, and Enterprise.

The principal expenses for new members were an initiation fee of from two to five dollars, annuals dues (with five dollars being the standard), and the purchase of a uniform. Each man was expected to appear ready for action on the field in proper shoes, pantaloons, shirt, cap, and belt. In an editorial in 1864 *Wilkes' Spirit* criticized the leading clubs for their shabby appearance in both practice games and interclub matches. It explicitly made the comparison between ball players and military troops by stating: "There is nothing to prevent a base-ball player's uniform from being as well known as that of a United States soldier." It added: "It is only requisite that each club should have a distinct style of cap, the pants and shirt can be the same for all, blue and white being the desirable colors. . . . But whether these colors are chosen, or gray or brown, is of secondary importance, so that each club owns a distinctive uniform; and, what is more, wears it all times on the ball-field."

Once these amateur clubs secured a suitable playing space, they scheduled practice days and arranged contests with rivals to provide their members with various types of competition. Most practiced two afternoons a week but not on Sundays. Saturdays brought hundreds of players to Boston Common, since many of that city's mercantile firms closed after lunch to permit their clerks to pursue their pastimes. Boston and Brooklyn also had several clubs that practiced in the early morning on weekdays, between five and seven o'clock. On exercise days the captain would make up sides from members who appeared on time, and if places remained open they would invite visitors on their grounds to join in the game. These scrimmages were used to select the club's first and second teams, with the worst players constituting a "muffin" squad.

Clubs also held special intrasquad matches, and their methods of choosing sides reveal traditional cultural distinctions that antebellum Americans drew among themselves. For both cricket and baseball clubs, by far the most common method was to match the married members ("Benedicts") against the single men ("Bachelors"). *Wilkes' Spirit* contrasted these playful encounters with the more serious interclub challenges: "These contests . . . are among the most enjoyable of the season, as the members meet on the ground more for recreation than for earnest work, time not being of so much importance in these matters as it is on occasions when the credit of the club is to be maintained against skillful opponents; more leisure being had, in the former case, for social intercourse, and of course for more genuine enjoyment." Another favorite pitted the heavyweights against the lightweights (literally), as in 1866 when Philadelphia's Keystone Fat Nine edged the Thins, 31–28. The city's *Sunday Dispatch* noted that the losers did not have a "ghost of a chance, and were driven from the field by the Falstaffs." The *Clipper* described the contest as "Fat and Greasy versus Lank and Leany"; it was a "very laughable game . . . which almost convulsed the lookers-on with merriment." Other intrasquad games matched seniors against juniors, with the division usually at thirty-two years of age. "Muffin" contests were exercises in ineptitude and provided amusement for participants and spectators alike. There were also a few political presidential campaign matches staged by the Chicago Excelsiors, including an 1860 encounter between the club's Stephen Douglas and Abraham Lincoln partisans and an 1868 game between the supporters of Ulysses Grant and Horatio Seymour. All of these show the spirit of playfulness in early amateur baseball, yet they also reveal significant personal, political, social, and athletic distinctions within organizations.

Since amateur sports clubs were social organizations, too, they scheduled periodic entertainment to supplement their regular business meetings and play days. The wealthiest club members hosted extravagant parties and fancy winter balls, while the middle-class white-collar and artisan associations held more modest affairs. Many clubs held annual dinners at the beginning and end of each season. Members and guests ate, drank, sang, told stories, and reminisced until the early morning hours. These social events were as popular among working-class clubs like the Brooklyn Eckfords as they were with the more affluent Knickerbockers. Some organizations even promoted intellectual pursuits, meeting in winter for debate, discussion, and fellowship.

While "muffins" and orators enjoyed their play days, parties, and meetings, the better athletes competed in interclub matches that generated excitement and promoted their sport. Before the Civil War many clubs fielded both first and second nines, but after 1865 there were fewer contests between reserves. Secretaries and match committees had the delicate task of issuing and responding to challenges for a "friendly game of ball." Normally, clubs preferred to play against those organizations with a similar age and social class membership. They also favored playing local rivals, although inter-city and even interstate contests were common, especially among clubs in the New York City vicinity. A few of the elite organizations, such as the Knickerbockers, restricted their play to other white-collar teams or those that shared their home grounds. Notwithstanding the above restrictions, antebellum baseball saw numerous interclass matches among both junior and senior players.

At most matches sportsmen observed traditional rituals and customs. After a baseball contest the president or captain of the defeated side invariably presented the game ball as a trophy to an official of the victorious team. Often it would be wrapped in gold foil, with the score and date of the game inscribed. Brief speeches accompanied this ceremony, as each side praised the sportsmanship and skill of the opposition. Sometimes special prizes or bouquets of flowers were awarded to the highest scoring batsmen. While the newspapers refer to a few challenges for prize money, most clubs condemned the idea of competing for cash. The post game dinner after most major baseball challenges could be quite elaborate. During the late 1850s this lavish socializing created sufficient tension, with clubs competing at the dinner table as well as on the field, that the NABBP recommended the abolition of refreshments after matches. Many people felt that the custom had degenerated into a practice that was "seriously detrimental to the interests of the game, owing to the spirit of emulation that arose among the clubs, each aspiring to excel each other in the expense and splendor of these entertainments."

The tradition persisted into the early 1860s in several cities, but after the Civil War these lavish dinners were no longer common. In New York City the leading clubs resolved in 1865 not to entertain each other at matches, although they felt obliged to give special attention to rivals from other cities. While on tour, the Philadelphia Athletics tried to discourage the home team from hosting expensive dinners or suppers, preferring simple refreshments after the game. When Brooklyn's Excelsior club wined and dined the Nationals of Washington, D.C., adding a sightseeing tour of the city, the *Clipper* noted the extravagant "palatial feasts" and criticized the team for violating "an express rule of the Association prohibiting this style of thing."

Informal matches, college games, and first nine interclub contests on the home front all heightened public awareness of baseball as it gained momentum during Civil War. Championship competition among the elite teams elevated the sport to a new level of popularity. As spectators flocked to featured games, the commercialization of baseball accelerated, bringing with it not only further rounds of growth for the national pastime, but also new and troubling issues concerning professionalism, gambling, poor sportsmanship, and spectator disorders. A new era for baseball dawned even before the last shots were fired in the epic battle between the North and South.

5

Championship Competition and Commercialization

In late June 1864 the Atlantics and the Mutuals began a series of matches that would determine which nine would claim the title of champions for that year. Although the Eckfords had held that honor for the previous two seasons, their first nine had suffered several key defections to their rivals, and the club delayed recruiting able substitutes until late in the summer. The *Clipper* regretted that only the Atlantics and the Mutuals appeared to be seriously contesting for the championship that summer. It explained that the importance attached to championship play forced clubs "to make such extra exertions to increase their playing strength that they come to monopolize material enough to make two or three good playing clubs." It specifically criticized the Atlantics and the Mutuals for having too many good players, "thus depriving other organizations of material that would greatly enlarge the circle of our first class playing clubs." That journal also lamented the increasing role of gamblers, pointing out that at feature matches "a class of individuals are introduced among the patrons of the game, and an objectionable influence brought to bear thereby, that seriously conflicts with the best interests of base ball, these influences being mainly such as . . . would bring the game down to a very low level."

The Atlantics regained the title they had last held in 1861 by sweeping two games from the Mutuals. They easily won the first encounter, 26–16, as the Mutuals had to rally for five runs in the bottom of the ninth inning "to save such of their friends from loss who had accepted offers of bets that the Atlantics would beat the Mutuals by a score of two to one." In late August the Mutuals kept their hopes for a pennant alive by dethroning the Eckfords by a count of 29–17. The teams played their return match on the grounds of the Atlantics in Bedford on September 12 in front of a crowd estimated by *Wilkes' Spirit* as numbering six thousand persons. A throwing error by the Mutuals' pitcher led to four unearned runs for the Atlantics in the first inning, but the Mutuals rallied to take a two run lead going into the seventh inning. However, their opponents outscored them ten to three over the last third of the game and triumphed, 21–16. *Wilkes' Spirit* praised the Mutuals for playing "in a handsome and expert manner," and remarked that the defeat "did not in the slightest degree dampen the ardor and confidence of the Mutuals in themselves." The game concluded with the traditional ritual wherein the Mutuals' captain, Billy McMahon, delivered the game ball to his counterpart on the Atlantics, "the 'war horse of base-ball,' Peter O'Brien." The Atlantics, as hosts, then treated their rivals to "a generous entertainment" as a "fitting *finale* to this exciting game." Among the stars of the Atlantics for this series and throughout 1864 were catcher Dickey Pierce, who in later seasons would be celebrated for his innovative play at shortstop, "Old Reliable" first baseman Joe Start, center fielder Peter O'Brien, and pitcher Tom Pratt, acquired from the Athletics the previous year.

Good will and sportsmanship prevailed in these contests and in the majority of intrasquad, practice, and interclub games played among less talented nines, but there is also evidence that controversy and hard feelings marred many early matches. Early baseball evolved on the home front during the war years in cities and towns that were divided by political factions, economic and labor conflicts, and racial, ethnic, religious, and social class tensions. Many of these political, economic, and social divisions shaped the development of early American baseball and appeared in interclub disputes and spectator disorders. This was especially true of those communities that witnessed the most significant gains in the new

15. Champions of America. Brooklyn Atlantics. The Atlantics claimed baseball championships in 1861, 1864, and 1865 as they defeated all challengers from the New York City region and Philadelphia during those years. They enrolled many butchers and others from the food preparation trades and had a large working class following. Library of Congress, Prints and Photographs Division.

national pastime: Brooklyn, Manhattan, Newark, Philadelphia, and Boston. While most citizens in the northeast were solidly behind the Union cause and the Republican Party, the Democrats also had a strong following in some areas, especially in New York City and New Jersey. The draft inevitably created conflicts between upper and middle class men who could afford to pay for substitutes to serve in the army, and those in the lower ranks who were forced to risk their lives in combat. Moreover, while military spending fueled economic prosperity throughout the region, certain groups and classes benefited more than others. Workers clashed with merchants and shop and factory owners, especially as inflation reduced their real wages.

A flood of Irish and German immigrants into northern cities during the 1840s and 1850s generated an escalation of nativist attacks against the newcomers, especially between Protestant groups and Catholics. Although African-Americans constituted only a small percentage of the populations of urban centers, their concentration in manual labor and service positions triggered racist resentment among poor whites who were competing with them for the lowest paying jobs. Ill will between the Irish and black residents sometimes flared into violence—most tragically during the murderous draft riots in New York City in July 1863.

Journalists regularly applauded exhibitions of good sportsmanship in the informal "muffin" and fun games discussed previously, but they also frequently criticized rude behavior, bad sportsmanship, and club disharmony. America's early players were raised in a culture that valued sport both for the recreation it provided them and also as a means to express group loyalty and friendly relations with rivals. Yet baseball games were also competitive events that stressed individual and group achievement as much as good manners. Inevitably, many of the stresses and strains of the society of this era were played out on the diamond. Club officials and sportswriters did encourage an atmosphere of amicable competition, but winning and losing still mattered a great deal. New York's junior teams, especially those in Brooklyn, were notorious for being quarrelsome. Senior clubs in several cities also exhibited hard feelings, both before and during the Civil War. An observer of the Philadelphia baseball boom argued that "petty jealousies, unmanly criticism, and childish bickerings, not only between rival clubs, but members of the same club . . . retard the popularity of the game, and injure the success of the clubs." Another Philadelphia sportsman asked: "When will the Philadelphia clubs learn that it is much more creditable to give up a ball with equanimity, than to fall into the manners and customs of blackguards? The club that cannot stand a defeat is unworthy of victory."

Among the many specific causes for such controversies and ill will, the most frequent were differences over access to grounds, the eligibility of players, rules and umpires' decisions, gambling and other forms of interference by spectators, and championship competition. In some cases one or more of these escalated existing class tensions among rivals. Organizations that shared the same playing field normally got along well, but there were exceptions. In Philadelphia, for example, bad blood between the Olympic and Athletic clubs was evident in 1862 when the latter team was deprived of its two days of play at Camac's Wood. One player charged that the Olympics had circulated reports that the Athletics had disbanded so as to bid for and obtain the field. The eligibility of players to participate in interclub matches sometimes led to heated exchanges. The National Association barred men from playing for more than one club, although this did not stop the practice or the complaints that ensued. In 1864 the *Brooklyn Daily Eagle* condemned the leading Philadelphia clubs for fielding members of other organizations in their matches. That paper criticized the practice as "utterly destructive" of the interest of those teams that played only their own men. It explained: "That *esprit du corps* [sic] from which emanates much of the interest of games club vs. club, and which so greatly contributes to the maintenance of club organizations, would no longer exist in any club were this custom to be generally adopted." Baseball also witnessed many controversies over umpires' verdicts. In 1858 *Porter's Spirit*, in discussing the settlement of disputes between players and umpires, advised sportsmen "to assume the referee to be *ever in the right*, and to bow to his decree whether it be *right or wrong*." An 1860 match between Philadelphia's Equity and Athletic clubs was marred by an argument over an umpire's decision, and again two years later theAthletics blamed their losses to the Olympics on the official, R.F. Stevens.

Another example of how a baseball game could produce ill will among the contestants occurred in Philadelphia in late July 1864. The Resolutes of Brooklyn were completing a three game tour of that city with a match against the home town Olympics. The game became intensely exciting in the ninth inning, when the visitors needed five runs to tie the Olympics. At that point the captain of the Olympics, Charles Bomeisler, dropped a fly ball that led to a run by the Resolutes. According to the *Clipper*, loud cheers from spectators who cared more about seeing a defeat of the Olympics than a victory by the visiting team contributed to the ugly scene that followed. That paper interpreted the crowd reaction as evidence of partisan feelings between the Athletics and Olympics, which reflected "more the spirit of two factions than of two reputable clubs of the base ball fraternity." Bomeisler then called "time" and ordered his men off of the field, claiming that it had become too dark to continue play. The crowd then gathered around the players and the umpire, and "over ten minutes were consumed in disgraceful wrangling." Finally the umpire ordered play to resume, with enough light remaining for the final outs to be recorded for a narrow one run triumph by the Olympics. The ending was most unpleasant for the Resolutes, for the newspaper reports of the game suggest that had there been no interruption of their batting it is likely that they would have triumphed. The *Clipper* and the *Brooklyn Daily Eagle* excoriated Bomeisler for his actions, even though he tried to make up for his misconduct by treating the Resolutes to a trip to Schuylkill Falls the next day. The *Eagle* described Bomeisler as "a wild, thoughtless, reckless, good-natured fellow, liberal as a patron of the game, and manly enough to acknowledge himself wrong when he is so, [who] . . . nevertheless acts at times as a prejudiced and bitter partisan as can be found in the base ball community."

Championship and all-star competition brought out both the best and the worst in wartime and postwar baseball. Club rivalries within cities, states, and regions certainly raised the standard of play and stimulated enthusiasm among players and spectators, but these special contests also produced much ill will and controversy, in part because of the unofficial nature of the titles. Custom dictated that whichever team won two out of three games from all of its rivals earned a championship. But in some cases club officials were unable (or unwilling) to schedule a deciding third match if the teams split the first two. In the absence of any strong governing body to regulate challenges, resolve disputes, and designate a winner, controversies multiplied.

The troubled relations among Brooklyn's three top teams— the Excelsiors, Atlantics, and Eckfords, best exemplifies the negative consequences for sportsmanship of these intense rivalries. The Excelsiors and the Eckfords suspended play with each other for many years after a dispute over the 1858 New York versus Brooklyn all-star series. The Atlantics and the Excelsiors were on better terms until a riotous scene at the third and deciding game of their 1860 championship series embittered their relations. The riot that ended the Atlantic–Excelsior series was symptomatic of the nativism and social class antagonism that troubled many communities—the Irish, working class Atlantics versus the Excelsior gentlemen, for example. A *Clipper* editorial identified the true cause of disorder as "the *spirit of faction* . . . in which the foreign element of our immense metropolitan population, and their native offspring, especially, delights to indulge." While noting that gambling contributed to the trouble, the paper stated that the real evil lay in "the bitterness of party spirit and sectional strife," in fire department fights, in lower-class gangs, and in sectarian religious jealousies. "In short," it continued, "whether it is 'our country,' 'our party,' 'our company,' 'our club,' or 'our church,' the same evil spirit rules the actions and paralyzes the virtuous tendencies of all who succumb to its baneful influence, replacing kindly feelings with bitter hared, and manly emulation and generous rivalry with revengeful retaliation." According to the *Clipper*, the remedy lay "in the self control of contending clubs and parties, and in a strict adherence to the rules that guide the actions of a man of honor and a gentleman." Of course, proper conduct among the contestants did not guarantee peace and quiet among the spectators. When issues of social class or nationality appeared, as they apparently did in the Atlantic–Excelsior matches of 1860, there was always the potential for problems in the crowd. In November of that year the *Clipper* called for more cordiality and friendship among Brooklyn's three leading teams, stating that "when the rivalry between clubs is carried to an extent that leads to mutual jealously and ill feeling, it is about time that matches should cease to be played." Four years later the *Brooklyn Daily Eagle* applauded the restoration of friendly relations among a number of clubs, and urged the Excelsiors, Atlantics, and Eckfords to bury their hatchets and resume their rivalries with friendly ball games. "It is time, gentlemen," it lectured the members, "that the boyish animosities which had led to your mutual estrangement should be succeeded by that manly forgiveness of past errors of conduct which ever characterizes the actions of men worthy of the name of gentlemen."

Although the problems with championship games became more apparent after the war was over, during the final two years of the conflict journalists were already commenting on the evil effects of championship encounters. In 1863 the *Brooklyn Daily Eagle* remarked: "The bitter rivalry that ensues, the objectionable efforts that are likely to be made to increase the playing strength of the contesting clubs, and the general discord that is thereby introduced, to say nothing of the evils arising from the encouragement that is also given to the gambling spirit by the opportunities afforded for betting in large amounts by means of these contests, afford sufficient proof of the injurious effect they have on the welfare of the game." The many incidents of ill will on ball fields prompted Henry Chadwick and other writers to complain that major contests lacked the "good humor and kindly feeling" so evident in the fun games played by "muffins," select nines of heavyweights, and others who were simply trying to amuse themselves. These journalists were disturbed that the encounters too closely resembled the more deadly contests on the battlefields of the then still ongoing Civil War. They were also upset that the games served the interests of gamblers rather than the lovers of true sport. As the *Eagle* remarked with regret in the fall of 1864: "first class matches, nowadays, instead of being meetings on the ball fields for recreation, in which good nature and fun are combined with the excitement of a lively game to create enjoyable sport, are transformed into serious trials of skill between contestants who are, in one respect, but the mere automatons on a mimic field of battle, handled for the pecuniary benefit and personal interests of an outside class, who care no more for the game, as a means of enjoyable exercise and recreation, than they do for the improvement of the equine stock of the country by means of the race courses, their sole motive being the gratification of their gambling propensities, at the expense of a manly pastime and healthful exercise." It concluded that "it is about time these serious, business-like contests should be changed to trials of skill, in which good humor and kindly feelings are the prevailing feature of the matches." But instead the postwar period would only accentuate the tendencies toward serious competition, commercialization, professionalism, and bureaucratization in baseball.

Championship matches attracted large crowds throughout the war years, and it is not surprising that sporting entrepreneurs and club officials soon realized that spectators would pay to see their favorite nines compete. Premier baseball matches attracted thousands of people, while even minor contests drew hundreds of fans. What explains the sport's power to generate such a high degree of public interest? Scholars and journalists have argued that the fascination with baseball today derives from its pastoral qualities, its scientific and statistical aspects, its capacity to evoke strong feelings of nostalgia for childhood and youth, its hero worship, its peculiar combination of individualism and teamwork, its analogy to war, and so on. Most of these theories come from people who have pondered the meaning of their favorite sport without really consulting those who pack the stadiums and watch the games on television. While it is hard to extract the essence of baseball's appeal from today's crowds and viewers, it is much more difficult to explain its popularity during its first few decades, as early spectators left scant records of their feelings toward baseball. Yet newspaper accounts of early ball games suggest that many of the forces that drew people to contests during the 1850s and 1860s are still important influences behind the attraction of modern baseball.

Before the war baseball clubs did not restrict attendance at their matches and did not charge an admission fee, except for a special all-star series between New York and Brooklyn at the Fashion Race Course in 1858. As a result, on Boston Common, at Camac's Wood in Philadelphia, at Hoboken's Elysian Fields, and at virtually all of the early ball fields, both blue- and white-collar workers and their families watched amateur antebellum baseball. But during the early 1860s entrepreneurs and club officials did begin to enclose fields and impose a price to witness major contests. They did so in part to exclude spectators from the poorer classes. Yet there is also considerable evidence that baseball games drew fans from a wide range of social groups even when an admission price was imposed. For example, many of those who came to the first of the ball games at the Fashion Race Course in 1858 were prosperous, arriving in fancy wagons and coaches. But apparently not all who watched the third and deciding contest were as well heeled, for according to *Porter's Spirit*, "a large deputation of overgrown boys from Brooklyn occupied a prominent position in the Grand Stand, and they materially interfered with the pleasure of the game by their noisy and very partial comments on the decisions of the Umpire, when unfavorable to the Brooklyn Nine." In describing the huge throng that attended an 1865 contest between the New York Mutuals and the Brooklyn Atlantics, the *Clipper* commented on the variety of people in attendance, with minority representation of "roughs," the "blackleg fraternity," and pickpockets.

People attended these early sporting events for widely different reasons and experienced the games in many different ways. Non-participating players from other clubs frequently appeared at important matches to observe the skills of their fellow athletes and future opponents. Sportswriters such as Henry Chadwick stressed the aesthetic appeal of "the beautiful game of baseball" and often presented a detailed critique of the quality of play, complimenting clever pitching, fine fielding, and strong batting. Charles King Newcomb, a Philadelphia man of letters, thought that baseball provided object lessons in art and science. He appreciated a pitcher's "statuesque posture" and wrote that the sport was also a "proof of physics": the "rush & lines of the balls in their passage though the air" reminded him of "the action of planetary orbs." Many spectators enjoyed hard hitting, while others appreciated the fine points of scientific batting and acrobatic fielding.

A major attraction of baseball was the excitement of the competition, especially for local, state, and national championships, coupled with the uncertainty of the outcome. The vicarious involvement of the spectators in the game was as obvious in the 1850s and 1860s as it is today. Every team had its "club followers," those who identified with their heroes and came to root them to victory—although sometimes they revealed their loyalties all too plainly. In the fall of 1861, when the Olympics and Athletics played a game for bragging rights in Philadelphia, the *Clipper* reported that "the manifest feeling among the spectators in favor of the Athletic nine was too marked for the good of future play."

Although undoubtedly there were many who flocked to these matches for the fine plays and the excitement of the competition, some certainly had a more pecuniary interest. Sports gambling already had a long history in America when the first modern baseball games were played. Not only did the public wager on these events; so did some of the contestants. During the 1850s clergymen and other leaders of public opinion continued to condemn gambling, yet the many references to wagering in the daily press seem to indicate that the public had come to tolerate it. More than a few people were still quite sensitive about the moral respectability of the new pastime, however. A contributor to *Porter's Spirit* was upset when that journal mentioned "very large bets" made on a contest between Brooklyn's Enterprise and Star junior teams. "Was it necessary to drag this in the newspapers," he asked, "in order to let the public know that ball-playing begins to assume some of the worst features of sport? I think not."

Wagering on baseball was a nearly universal practice during the sport's formative years, even though the NABBP prohibited participants from betting. It had no means of enforcing such bans, however, especially since many of the New York area clubs and the large majority of those from other states were not even members of the National Association. It is true that whenever gambling produced ugly incidents at contests, some of the prominent clubs passed resolutions against the practice. But their actions did not prevent New York's spectators from placing their bets, and many players probably continued to wager in private as well. In Massachusetts, much money was at stake on the result of a championship match in 1859 between the Unions of Medway and the Winthrops of Holliston. When the new Hamilton Club of Jersey City challenged the Newark Adriatics in 1858, "any amount of 'lucre' could be had on the defeat of the Hamiltons." After the Mechanics of Jersey City defeated the Resolutes of Brooklyn in September 1860, one of the losers complained about "the free flourish of money, shaken in the faces of bystanders and the loud and frequent offers to bet upon the game, together with the low and profane language used." A spokesman for the Mechanics charged that a supporter of the Resolutes had opened the wagering, and he asked if that club "would like to undertake to stop outsiders from betting on the game?" "If they do," he wrote, "I think they will get more kicks and cuffs than pence." As long as ball games had winners and losers, little could be done to stop gambling.

For promoters of the national pastime, the greatest threat to the integrity of the sport was the fixing of matches by gamblers and bribed players. In 1865 a special investigating committee of New York's Mutual club accused William Wansley of splitting one hundred dollars with two teammates, Edward Duffy and Thomas Devyr. Devyr admitted that before the contest against the Brooklyn Excelsiors, Wansley asked him to join in the conspiracy for thirty dollars. He testified that Wansley said, "We can lose this game without doing the Club any harm, and win the home-and-home game. . . . Now, you ain't got a cent, nor neither has Duffy; you can make this money without any one being a bit the wiser of it." After Wansley assured Devyr that he would not have to do the actual "heaving" of the match himself, the latter agreed. The three men were subsequently expelled from the club but were reinstated in 1867 (Devyr), 1868 (Duffy), and 1870 (Wansley).

While this incident remains the only documented example of a fixed contest during this period, there was much suspicion that many matches might have been lost intentionally. The sporting and daily newspapers of the half decade following the Civil War are filled with speculation that the Atlantics, the Athletics, the Mutuals, and other prominent teams sometimes dropped games to set up a third, deciding contest, which would bring higher gate receipts and more bets. Some people charged that these clubs sold games outright for the benefit of gamblers' rings. But since the outcome of these games was so uncertain, and since it was so difficult to obtain proof of wrongdoing, the extent of corruption was never clear. Of all the opponents of gambling and bribery, none was more outspoken or energetic than Henry Chadwick. He supported the honest professional player but conceded that by "making the game a means of livelihood, he becomes a more prominent object for the attack of the blacklegs." Chadwick's solution was "to prohibit betting of large sums in connection with every fairly contested game." Of course, neither the NABBP nor any other organization had the power to stop or control wagering on baseball.

While the artistry of players, the excitement of competition, and the chance to profit were all major attractions of early American team sports, many people also enjoyed the spectacles provided by the leading events. As historian Warren Goldstein has pointed out, there were important similarities between the cultures of baseball and the theater during this era. The sportsmen played out the drama of a match on their special stage, dressed in costumes that symbolized their club affiliation. Like the world of the theater, baseball had associations with both respectable society and the less-reputable life of Victorian popular amusements. People flocked to games for many of the same reasons they attended plays produced for the masses; their tastes were both high-brow and low-brow. Some simply wanted to watch an exciting contest on a beautiful day, while others anticipated a good time spiced with some liquor and wagering. A match between two prominent clubs or an all-star contest played on a sunny day before an enthusiastic audience produced quite a show. When the best players of New York and Brooklyn met for their first game at the Fashion Race Course in 1858, *Porter's Spirit* reported that "no race day the Fashion Course has ever seen, presented such a brilliant numerical array. . . . the *coup d'oeil* . . . was brilliant in the extreme." Artists and photographers, including Matthew Brady, and illustrators employed by Currier and Ives often attended the feature matches to capture these novel scenes for those unable to witness them in person. The special events that drew thousands of spectators produced a carnival atmosphere, as the great crowds attracted con artists, traders, vendors, and thieves. At the Fashion Race Course series, spectators arriving at the entrance encountered "thimble-riggers and card sweaters" who were trying to swindle a few dollars out of the "greenies." At the second game between the Atlantics and the Excelsiors in August 1860, on the outskirts of a huge throng of onlookers were "various itinerant tradesmen and vendors of eatables and drinkables." Fans crowded into fancy colored tents to quench their thirst with beer or stronger spirits, such as "Jersey lightning," which increased the business of the police force. Pickpockets plagued these and other contests, prompting newspapers to report their activities and warn people to be on the alert.

The presence of female spectators at baseball and cricket matches proved that the two sports had achieved respectability, but it is doubtful that the women really inspired the players or restrained the hecklers, gamblers, and rowdies. Their attendance had little impact on those spectators who liked to be active and vocal during the games. Heated rivalries generated much emotion, which led to physical and verbal interference and fighting by club followers and assorted troublemakers. Baseball players and club managers were sensitive to the problem of crowd control and attempted to cope with it by appeals to the spectators, which usually worked. Some of the Brooklyn baseball clubs owned their own grounds and hired police to maintain order and remove objectionable persons. The Excelsiors enjoyed a reputation for preserving peace at their field in South Brooklyn, while the Atlantics of Bedford did not control their grounds and therefore had trouble with unruly spectators. On a few occasions, such as the deciding game of the Atlantic–Excelsior series in 1860, even the police were unable to restrain the crowd.

During the amateur era, most of the baseball matches were played on open grounds. When thousands appeared to witness a contest, clearing the field of spectators was no easy task, and keeping them away from the players during the game could also be difficult. Generally the crowd cooperated by staying behind lines marked as bounds, but sometimes club followers got too close to the action— for example, outfielders might have to retrieve balls from among a forest of legs. During Philadelphia's first summer of baseball in 1860, police were hired to keep spectators away from the base lines, but at one game a local paper reported "quite a crowd backing up the third base" and complained that "players on the second base are frequently at a loss to know whether the third base is occupied or not."

More common and annoying than physical interference was heckling. Prominent sportswriters blamed gamblers for instigating many instances of verbal abuse by spectators, which irritated the umpire, the players, and others in the crowds. A *Clipper* reporter (probably Henry Chadwick) believed that "these outside parties, these excrescences of ball matches . . . are generally the very persons that create all the trouble and ill feeling that ever occurs on these occasions." He continued:

> Many of the spectators at ball matches assume to themselves the power belonging solely to the captains and umpires, directing players how to act, and loudly deciding upon points of the game as umpires, not according to the merits of the questions, but solely in reference to their peculiar wishes as to the result. From this source has arisen the complaints made by clubs of different localities, that they cannot visit this or that ground without having to encounter the opposition of a large delegation of "club followers" as well as the nine of the club they play with, the former invariably being the parties most to be feared.

Fights and other disturbances among boys and men also created problems for baseball clubs. In July 1860 a Jersey City resident reported that "spectators are seriously annoyed on the Hamilton's grounds by the misconduct and noise of rude and rowdyish boys." He urged officials "to see that good order is preserved, and that the nuisance caused by groups of yelling, hooting and wrestling boys mixing themselves with the quiet spectators, and sometimes insulting the visiting clubs, be prevented." The *Daily Courier and Advertiser* suggested that "a policeman be engaged to keep order among the noisy and ill-bred urchins who intrude themselves among the spectators and annoy and disturb every one in the vicinity with bad language and rough conduct." This advice was apparently not followed, for one month later the same newspaper noted that a contest was "marred as usual by the misconduct of a set of rowdies whom there was no policeman present to keep in check." In Philadelphia, a game between the Equity and Winona nines was disturbed by "the very reprehensible conduct of a number of small boys, who, by shouting and running between the bases distracted the attention of the players." An old-timer from the City of Brotherly Love remembered that in the 1860s the conduct of the players was excellent, but he recalled many nasty melees among the spectators after the games. He was among those who followed "an adherent of the Atlantics . . . several blocks to a drugstore where his wounds from gunshot were treated." He reported: "Near-riots were frequently the results of clashes between hucksters and drivers who on top of their vehicles in Columbia av. hurled remarks at each other until these ended in fistic encounters. But this was all off the field of honor."

The commercialization of baseball followed naturally from the long-accepted practice of charging admission fees for popular amusements in general and sporting events (such as horse racing) in particular. There were even precedents for putting a price, ranging from ten to fifteen cents, on ball games. Examples are the New York versus Brooklyn all-star matches held at the Fashion Race Course in 1858, the contests between select Manhattan and Philadelphia cricket teams and the touring all-England eleven in 1859, the St. George Cricket Club's regular games in 1860, and the benefits held by cricket clubs to reward their professionals. But these were clearly exceptions to the prewar custom of free admission. After 1861, however, promoters translated the popular appeal of the new national game into commercial profits.

During the 1860s there were several ways of establishing a baseball business. The first involved capitalists who enclosed and improved a ground, which they offered rent-free to clubs in exchange for the right to charge an admission fee for premier matches. William H. Cammeyer inaugurated this practice in 1862 when he drained his winter skating pond for summer baseball and opened the Union grounds in Brooklyn's eastern district. Cammeyer and his associates had initially intended to found a "Union Skating, Riding

School, Base Ball, Gymnastic and Boating Association," but were forced to scale down their plans because of the hard times brought on by the war. Cammeyer contracted with the Eckford, Putnam, and Constellation clubs, granting each the right to use the Union Grounds for two days a week. A six foot fence bordered the property, with new facilities that included a long wooden shed capable of accommodating several hundred persons, benches for ladies, standing and sitting room for 12,000–15,000 spectators, and a "large and commodious club house" for members of the three clubs. Cammeyer originally intended to collect rent from baseball clubs for use of the grounds, but he then switched to the practice of charging for admission, with the gate receipts (25–50 cents for feature matches) divided between himself and the clubs. Band music (including the "Star Spangled Banner") and an exhibition game highlighted the opening day's festivities on May 15, which attracted several thousand spectators, including representatives from several nines of Brooklyn and Manhattan. Newspaper reporters praised the new ballpark, especially because they believed that it would improve crowd control and encourage more female attendance at important games. The *Brooklyn Daily Eagle* remarked approvingly: "The chief object of the [Union] Association is to provide a suitable place for ball playing, where ladies can witness the game without being annoyed by the indecorous behavior of the rowdies who attend some of the first-class matches." The Union grounds became the home field for the Eckfords and the Mutuals (who left Hoboken after the war), and the Atlantics joined them in 1868. It remained the center of baseball in New York City until 1878.

Cammeyer's success prompted Reuben Decker and a partner, Hamilton Weed, to follow his example. They converted their skating facility into the Capitoline Grounds in Brooklyn's western district in May 1864, contracting with the Atlantic and Enterprise clubs, who agreed to use the field for four days each on alternate weeks. In 1865 the *New York Herald* rated the Capitoline Grounds "the most extensive and complete ball grounds in the United States." Unlike Cammeyer, Decker and Weed prohibited public gambling at their park, although they had no means of preventing

private betting. Their facility, named after the ancient Roman celebration of the Capitoline games, included a large hall adjacent to
the field for the entertainment of visiting clubs. While the Atlantics had a sentimental attachment to the Capitoline Grounds because they had played their first games at that location prior to the
war, they did defect to the greener pastures of the Union Grounds
in 1868.

During and after the war a few entrepreneurs in the New
York region and also across the country organized all-star contests,
charity events, or tournaments, offering prize money to the participating clubs and charging spectators to see the action. A few clubs,
like the Athletics and Olympics of Philadelphia, tried a third
method of commercializing baseball when they rented or purchased
their own field, built a fence, and set an admission fee for matches.
In 1864 the Olympics leased a large space from the city of Philadelphia north of the Spring Garden Reservoir at the intersection of
Jefferson and twenty-fifth streets. The members raised $1500 to
build a clubhouse and improve the ground, which they agreed to
share with the Athletics and Mercantiles. Like Cammeyer, they
demonstrated their patriotism and loyalty to the United States by
naming their field the "Union Ball Grounds of Philadelphia."

The commercialization of baseball during and after the Civil
War did not bring about any drastic changes in the behavior of spectators. Some promoters and enthusiasts thought that the trend toward enclosed grounds and admission fees ranging from ten to fifty
cents for most games would lead to more select and well-mannered
crowds. But this was not usually the case, in part because many people from the lower classes were willing to pay to see feature events.
Also, thousands of fans congregated outside the fences and often
found ways to view the sport over or through the barriers. Sometimes
they created a distraction. *Wilkes' Spirit* reported that at a game between the Brooklyn Eckfords and the Unions of Morrisania (Bronx,
NY) in October 1862, "the boys outside of the grounds upon the
embankment caused a great deal of disturbance and noise, their bad
conduct annoying the players of both clubs—more particularly, the
Union Nine." It commented: "We are aware that it is about a diffi-

cult a job to subdue these 'Young Eckfords' and embryo ball players, as it would be to suggest that a few officers might quiet them somewhat, and perhaps develop less pugnacity in their dispositions." Charging admission to enclosed fields did lead to better accommodations for ladies, the press, and the general public, but it did not eliminate fan interference, fights in the stands, or crowd disorders on the fields. Henry Chadwick chastised the daily press for reporting prizefights in detail, arguing that this encouraged "those, who, in a crowd of spectators at a ball match, at the cry of 'fight, fight,' rush from the manly excitements of such a contest to seek gratification for their brutal tastes in witnessing and encouraging bloody encounters between two or three blackguards." People who paid twenty-five or fifty cents for admission also fought over good seats and were enraged when others blocked their view or that of their lady friends.

The commercialization of baseball naturally also stimulated professionalism in the sport. Despite the NABBP's ban on payment to participants, before and during the Civil War a few premier players accepted some form of compensation, including gifts, jobs, or direct payments. Perhaps the first two in this group were James Creighton and Al Reach. The Brooklyn Excelsiors very likely at least partially subsidized Creighton when they recruited him in 1860. In 1863 Al Reach became the object of an early baseball bidding war when several clubs offered him money to defect from the Eckfords of Brooklyn. Although Arthur P. Gorman of Baltimore (a future NABBP president and United States Senator) promised him the highest pay, Reach chose to compete for the Athletics of Philadelphia because it was closer to his home in Flushing, New York.

Certain organizations also staged annual benefit contests, with the gate receipts distributed among a few designated (and presumably needy) contestants. In November 1861 the *Clipper* criticized a game arranged between two picked nines of Brooklyn on the enclosed cricket ground in Hoboken to benefit Dicky Pierce of the Atlantics and Creighton of the Excelsiors. According to that journal, the game was entirely devoid of interest because what was at stake was not "the honor derived from a creditable victory," but rather "self interest, in a pecuniary point of view," which it viewed as an element "that is undoubtedly injurious, in its results, to the best interests of the game." In 1863 the *Brooklyn Eagle* detected an early trend toward professionalism by noting that "some have even intimated that ballplaying has become quite a money making business, many finding it to pay well to play well." The following year that paper defined three classes of players by skill level, not by compensation: professionals [most proficient]; amateurs [average players]; and muffins [novices]. It explicitly stated that "the professionals are, of course not such as those in cricket, that is, they are not paid for their services like cricket professionals, the rules of base ball strictly prohibiting anything of the kind." But within a few years the sporting weeklies and daily papers were reporting that several clubs were subsidizing a few players through one means or another. In 1865 those men could realize some cash benefit from being ball players, but their incomes were probably not significantly higher than the average skilled worker.

During the Civil War era thousands of men, women, and children from diverse social, ethnic, and racial backgrounds played or watched baseball games. Some created formal clubs, while others participated more informally in impromptu contests on vacant lots. The more serious competitors and associations engaged in championship competition, which spurred developments in commercialism and professionalism. Ill will among certain clubs and spectator disorders at several matches reflected the tensions of the age. As they competed the participants were not unmindful of the battles between northern and southern armies that would determine the fate of the union, but they did not allow the military emergency to spoil their athletic entertainment. As four long years of conflict drew to a close, these pioneers of early American baseball looked hopefully to a future that would provide a more fruitful environment in which their favorite sport could grow. The remaining task is to examine the legacy of the war for baseball, the new national pastime.

6

The War's Legacy

I n April 1865 northern baseball players looked forward to both the imminent collapse of the Confederacy and also a brilliant new season of action. As they rejoiced that four years of terrible carnage were coming to an end, they greeted the return of spring by flocking to ball fields instead of battlefields. But before they could properly inaugurate practice and competition for the season they had to cope with the shock of the assassination of Abraham Lincoln. Several clubs in Manhattan, Brooklyn, Philadelphia, and other northern cities postponed their opening days out of respect for the memory of the slain president, but after a brief period of mourning they returned to their diamonds. In Brooklyn the Exercise Club had a good turnout on the Saturday after Lincoln was shot, but suspended play until after his burial, and ordered that its flag be lowered to half-mast. Others followed suit, as the *Brooklyn Daily Eagle* reported: "all classes thus do honor to our deceased President." The Mutuals had planned a grand opening gala day on April 17 on the Elysian Fields in Hoboken, but *Wilkes' Spirit* reported that the recreation was adjourned *sine die*, as "a feeling of sadness and unfeigned sorrow pervaded the breast of every member." In Philadelphia the Mercantiles passed a series of resolutions "expressive of the feelings of the members concerning our late President and the terrible event by which the country was deprived of his priceless life." At the end of the month the *Daily Eagle* somberly noted: "Now that the general depression incident upon the funeral obsequies has somewhat sub-sided, Base Ball clubs will go to work more in good earnest."

That spring few if any of baseball's enthusiasts could have predicted the fantastic success or the host of difficulties it would experience over the next half-decade. But they were excited about their prospects for recreation and competition in a climate of peace rather than war. A report from the Equity club of Philadelphia noted that it was forced to suspend operation during the war as nearly all men of its first nine served on the "tented field," but "now the rebellion is crushed, we intend to take the field again." In New York City the *Clipper* hoped that former champion nines, such as the Atlantics, Excelsiors, and Eckfords, would retire to allow new challengers to contest for baseball supremacy. That sporting weekly argued that it was in the interest of the game and the leading clubs that no one team dominate, "otherwise, instead of a dozen or two of first-class clubs, we should soon have but three or four rival organizations to contend for the palm of victory; besides which, such a monopoly of success would prevent rising young clubs from striving to reach the same point of excellence, owing to the overpowering strength of their giant adversaries." But although the Excelsiors did bow out of the championship competition, the Atlantics and Eckfords remained contenders, as did the Mutuals, the Athletics, and eventually the Red Stockings of Cincinnati and the White Stockings of Chicago.

Baseball fever infected players of all ages, races, and levels of skill. While the famed Atlantics, Athletics, Mutuals, and other first-class nines battled to be recognized as the champions of the United States, lesser known teams of all shapes and sizes emulated their heroes on the ball fields of urban and rural America. In 1866 Philadelphia's *Sunday Mercury* proclaimed that "baseball is truly a national game, and not confined exclusively to Young America. . . . we have had our 'Fat and Thin' matches; the 'Ponies and Muffins' have given us a touch of their quality, and the 'Broken-winded Nine' of a prominent club have come in for a share of base ball honors, but they dwindle into insignificance when compared with the efforts of the 'Invalids.' "

During the immediate postwar years baseball experienced impressive growth in most sections of the United States. From the rocky coast of Maine to the Golden Gate of California, from upstart Chicago to the reconstructed states of Dixie, a baseball mania swept the land. The Civil War contributed significantly to the game's rapid expansion during the late 1860s, although baseball's popularity prior to 1861 provided the sport with a foundation that made it highly likely that it would grow rapidly after the return of peace. In addition, baseball played a major role in fostering nationalism in general and sectional reconciliation between North and South in particular during the early years of Reconstruction. However, although baseball promoted democratic values and equality in the nation for white Americans, it failed to enhance equal opportunity for African-Americans or improve their relations with whites.

During the immediate postwar period public officials took notice of the increasing popularity of baseball among the masses. As the *Clipper* observed: "Base Ball has undoubtedly become an institution of the country. . . . Politicians are commencing to curry favor with the fraternity of ball players, as a class of 'our fellow citizens' worthy the attention of 'our influential men, you know.' " Although Lincoln did not live long enough to formally acknowledge the elevated status of the game, his successor, Andrew Johnson, gave official presidential recognition to baseball in August 1865 when he received a delegation of visitors at the White House which included the Brooklyn Atlantics, Arthur P. Gorman (Postmaster of the U.S. Senate and President of the Washington Nationals), and sportswriter Henry Chadwick. After Gorman personally introduced each of the Atlantics to Johnson, Chadwick expressed his disappointment that the president had not attended the recent tournament in which the Atlantics had routed the hometown Nationals. Johnson replied that he regretted not being able to witness the game, pleading the pressure of official business. Chadwick then expressed his hope that Johnson would attend a future game that the Brooklyn Excelsiors had scheduled in Washington in September, "if but for a few minutes, as such countenance of the game would give a national stamp to it, which would greatly promote its popularity." Chadwick clearly believed that a presidential endorsement of the new sport would give a valuable boost to baseball across the country. At first, in 1866, Gorman received permission from Johnson to enlarge a building on the President's Grounds for storage of baseball equipment. And then, in August of the following year the Mutuals of New York traveled to Washington to play the Nationals. Before the game they elected Johnson an honorary member of their club and visited him at the White House. This time the president rewarded them by watching the contest, which the Mutuals won easily, 40–16. There is no record of the position of the Mutuals (still connected with Boss Tweed's Democratic Tammany Hall) on Johnson's Reconstruction policies, but one can speculate that their officers sided with him in his battles with the Radical Republicans in Congress.

Many baseball historians have stressed the importance of the army experience in popularizing the sport after the war, but it should also be emphasized that many men who enjoyed the game prior to the war but never served in the military helped to promote the sport in the cities to which they relocated after the conflict. The *Clipper* declared in 1865 that "when soldiers were off duty, base ball was naturalized in nearly every state in the Union, and thus extended in popularity," and it is true that the pastime remained popular among troops stationed in the West and South after 1865. For example, baseball clubs representing two army companies in Kansas competed on a spot "in the heart of the hunting grounds of the wild plains Indians, whose scalps we were then seeking." But civilians also did their share in nationalizing the game. Former residents of Philadelphia and Washington, D.C., for example, organized the first game of baseball ever played in Fayetteville, Tennessee, in October 1868, as the KKK club defeated "nine Carpetbaggers." The brief report of this game in the *Clipper* gives no clue concerning the composition of the sides, but it would appear that southern men connected with the Ku Klux Klan in that town squared off against northerners. Contestants in an 1868 match between Macon and Savannah, Georgia clubs included former members of New York City, Newark, Irvington, and Philadelphia nines. "Aleck" Pearsall,

116

who competed for the Brooklyn Excelsiors before he defected to the Confederacy, wound up after the war with the Montgomery Club of Alabama. A group of Washingtonians wandered "the land of gold and silver, found it impossible to forget their old pastime," and formed the Star City Club of Eastern City, Nevada, in 1870. Philadelphians in San Francisco founded four clubs before the Cincinnati Red Stockings arrived there on tour in 1869.

The spread of baseball after the war to former Confederate states is striking, with notable activity in several cities in Virginia and Texas and a real passion for the game in New Orleans. In Lynchburg, Virginia, Charles W. Button, a prominent editor and newspaper publisher, became an ardent booster of the sport in his town, claiming that Robert E. Lee had approved of baseball. With Button's encouragement the people of Lynchburg founded at least four clubs in 1867, including one composed of federal soldiers stationed there. At the University of Virginia in Charlottesville students organized a club soon after the war, while in Richmond at least fifteen adult and a dozen junior nines competed by the end of 1866. Henry Chadwick must have been pleased to see the rise of baseball in Richmond, considering his family ties to the former capital of the Confederacy and his failed attempts to introduce ball sports there prior to the war. The presence of federal troops occupying Richmond probably contributed to baseball's popularity in that city, and there was at least one game played between a local club and a team of Union soldiers stationed at Camp Grant.

A western variation of the Doubleday myth held that the Union Major General re-enacted his Cooperstown creation in Texas when he laid out the first baseball diamond in Galveston and organized the first match there on Washington's Birthday, 1867 with a contest between two sides of Union troops. While it is true that Doubleday did serve with the Freedmen's Bureau in Galveston at that time, it is highly unlikely that he played any role in the founding of baseball in that city. A more reliable account of the origins of baseball in Galveston describes a game played there in 1865 on a parade ground between "crack teams of the different regiments" quartered on vacant lots outside of town. According to a story about that match a group of local "ragamuffins and boys on the Island" watched the contest and then charged that the Yankees had "stolen our old game of 'townball' and substituted a few additional features." Soon thereafter the best team in Galveston was named after Robert E. Lee. Baseball had already been established in Houston prior to the war, and the game flourished after the conflict in both Texas towns.

Baseball had already become popular in New Orleans before Fort Sumter, and it is highly likely that the occupation by federal troops in 1862 helped to promote the game in that city. As previously discussed, federal prisoners held in New Orleans before it was occupied by Union soldiers later played baseball in other prison camps in the Confederacy. At the end of 1867 a correspondent to Chadwick's *Ball Players' Chronicle* reported: "Base Ball is in the zenith of its glory here. Every suitable ground is occupied by clubs composed of young and old, large and small, and from the most respectable families. On the ball field you meet the merchant, the clerk, the mechanic, members of the Press, and the student, all anxious to avail themselves of the amusement it affords, and derive benefit from the exercise. The match games are witnessed by thousands, with a good sprinkling of the fair sex."

Regional rivalries and intersectional matches accelerated the national growth of baseball and also had a significant impact on North–South relations during the postwar period. Once the eastern clubs began a series of long-distance tours via railroads and steamships, western and southern nines followed suit. In 1867 the Nationals of Washington, D.C., ventured beyond the Alleghenies and electrified western towns with a nine composed mostly of government clerks, lawyers, and students. They covered five states, traveling over 3,000 miles by train and boat at a cost of more than $5,000. Club officials, friends, and baseball reporters joined this pioneer barnstorming excursion, which became the prototype for future sporting tours. The following year the Atlantics, Athletics, and the Unions of Morrisania swept through the Midwest, creating a sensation in Pittsburgh, Cincinnati, Louisville, Indianapolis, St. Louis, Chicago, Buffalo, Cleveland, Detroit, Milwaukee, Forest City and Bloomington, Illinois, and elsewhere. Midwestern clubs also took to the road, journeying east for return matches with the great teams of New York, Brooklyn, Newark, and Philadelphia. New Orleans's Southern club was greeted upon its return from a western swing in 1869 by a grand torchlight procession of local clubs, a band, and a crowd of enthusiastic citizens. A local reporter wrote that the trip gave "a new impulse to base ball in our city." The Cincinnati Red Stockings' 1869 tour to California via the newly completed transcontinental railroad was the most ambitious and successful of all, as they capped an undefeated season with lopsided victories in the San Francisco region.

Some observers viewed the introduction or revival of baseball in the border and southern states as a positive force in reuniting the nation after the Civil War. In 1865 the *Clipper* noted that "Maryland [was] fast being reconstructed on this base-is" and hoped to see that state as the " 'Centre field' of our National game," adding that "there would have been fewer 'hands lost' and 'foul balls' had this been the case four years ago." While declaring that "base ball fever is rapidly assuming the form of an epidemic among the constructed and reconstructed denizens of the former stronghold of the extinct Divisocracy [Richmond, Va.]," the journal scolded the southerners of the Richmond club for refusing the challenge of the city's Union nine, which was composed of businessmen and federal officials. It stated: "We regret to learn of such petty feeling and sectional animosity being evinced by any party of Southern gentlemen calling themselves ball players. Our national game is intended to be national in every sense of the word, and, until this example was set by the 'Richmond Club,' nothing of a sectional character has emanated from a single club in the country."

Northern and southern journalists believed that the tours of the great eastern ball clubs would help to heal the bitter wounds of war. When the Nationals of Washington, D.C., visited Brooklyn in July 1866, the Excelsiors treated them to a lavish dinner, in violation of an NABBP rule prohibiting expensive entertainment. The *Clipper* viewed the Nationals as special guests from the south, despite the club's name and the connection of many of its members with the federal government. That paper argued that the Brooklynites' extravagance showed that "the ball players' 'policy of reconstruction' is one marked by true fraternal regard, irrespective of all political opinions or sectional feelings, the National Association knowing . . . 'No North, no South, no East, no West,' but simply the interest and welfare of the game itself, and the cultivation of kindly feelings between the different clubs." The Excelsiors also treated the Nationals to a tour of the sights of Brooklyn, which featured a pilgrimage to the monument the Excelsiors had erected in Greenwood Cemetery in honor of their deceased superstar, James Creighton. The entourage paid "silent but eloquent tribute to the memory of the greatest ball player ever known, some culling green mementos from his grave."

When the Nationals journeyed to Louisville, Kentucky in 1867, however, the hometown crowd viewed them as invading Yankees. *Wilkes' Spirit* reported that "a crowd of the most unruly partizan [*sic*] boors and rowdy boys" gave them a greeting that "was not at all in accordance with the reputation for chivalric sentiments which the Southern cities have hitherto claimed." The newspaper singled out female spectators for special criticism and urged that all sectional feeling be kept out of the game. It maintained: "were any Southern club to visit the North, it would be the pride of the Northern ladies to show the strangers a courteous reception. The Nationals . . . though from the shores of the Potomac, had too much of the North about them apparently to merit the favor of Southern women." Chadwick's *Ball Players' Chronicle* agreed that "the latitude of the home of the Nationals was too far *North* to elicit the impartial award of approbation which a club from some more Southern locality would have received."

As the 1860s drew to a close, excursions of ball clubs generated friendlier feelings and more hope that baseball could help bind north and south together. A reporter who praised the growing popularity of the sport in the South thought that more clubs in that region would follow the example of the touring Nationals. He believed that "more good will be done in the way of social reconstruction in a few seasons than the politicians could achieve in half a century." During the summer of 1868 the Athletics received a warmer reception in Louisville, and Philadelphia's *Sunday Mercury* defended the Louisville players and their gray uniforms, which "had been held up to scorn, and those who wear it denounced as rebels." Its reporter from the City of Brotherly Love "did not inquire the political status of the Louisville Club," not caring "whether they were former rebels or Union men because that "has got nothing to do with our National Game." He concluded: "if Jefferson Davis, or any other man who had served in the rebel cause, was to meet me on the ball field, and salute me as a gentleman, I would endeavor to prove to him that I was one."

In 1869 a New Orleans newspaper announced the upcoming trip of its Southern club to Memphis and St. Louis with players who "organized during the war while prisoners of war at Johnson's Island." Its editor wondered, along with his northern counterparts: "If the Southerns could be induced to visit New York and measure skill with the Atlantics and Mutuals, would it not be pleasant to see the hatchet buried in the great national game, spite of the efforts of politicians to keep up ill feeling between the sections?" *Wilkes' Spirit*, reporting on the Mutuals' December trip to New Orleans, observed: "This National Game seems destined to close the National Wounds opened by the late war. It is no idle pastime which draws young men, separated by two thousand miles, together to contest in friendship, upon fields but lately crimsoned with their brothers' blood in mortal combat." The Mutuals' twenty day trip to New Orleans, organized and financed by Boss William Tweed at a cost of $1800, resulted in a five game sweep for the New Yorkers and a modest boost for baseball in the south.

As baseball enthusiasts, journalists, and touring nines spread the gospel of the new pastime across America, national, state, and local sports organizations attempted to guide the game's growth. The New York City based NABBP acted in a number of ways to recognize and encourage regional and national expansion. It voted to rotate the annual meeting site among several cities, including Philadelphia (1867), Washington, D.C. (1868), and Boston (1869), making its conventions accessible to more players and clubs. It also elected officials from a variety of cities in a conscious attempt to broaden representation. In 1866 the *Clipper* urged the selection of Arthur P. Gorman of the Washington Nationals (a native of Howard County, Maryland and a former page and postmaster of the U.S. Senate) as the new NABBP president. It argued that in view of the ongoing reconstruction debate, "the [baseball] fraternity should prove to the world that sectionalism is unknown in our national game." Since "for the first time the South will enter the convention," the paper maintained, "the election of the president of the 'Champion Club of the South' would go far to prove the absence of any narrow sectional ideas in the National Association." The convention did choose Gorman as president and later greeted southern delegates with loud applause.

The Civil War had a momentous impact on race relations in all areas of life in the United States, including recreation and sports in general, and baseball in particular. The Emancipation Proclamation of 1863 and the postwar Thirteenth, Fourteenth, and Fifteenth Amendments to the Constitution raised issues of freedom and equal opportunity in American society that extended to the nation's ball fields. During the early Reconstruction era black ball players shared in the mania for the new national pastime, but they experienced only very limited success in gaining respect and equal treatment from their white counterparts.

Baseball fever swept through the African-American communities of many cities and towns during the 1860s, as all-black nines appeared in Newark, Camden, and New Brunswick, (NJ), Boston, Chicago, Rockford (IL), Ripley (OH), Washington, D.C., Harrisburg, Pittsburgh, Philadelphia, and Carlisle (PA), Brooklyn, New York, Utica, Buffalo, Niagara Falls, Albany, Rochester, Johnstown, and Lockport (NY), Baltimore, and New Orleans, among other places. Some of these clubs, such as Philadelphia's Pythians, recruited from the upper ranks of black society, while others enlisted men of lower status—for example, the Chicago Blue Stockings were hotel and restaurant waiters.

The Pythians merit special attention because of their prominence among black clubs during the formative years of black baseball, and also because of their efforts to gain acceptance among their white peers in the baseball fraternity of Philadelphia. While they ranked far below white players in social status, they were among the black elite of their city. Two-thirds were natives of Pennsylvania (compared to 40 percent of the total black population of Philadelphia) and one-fifth were born in Virginia or South Carolina. Their mean age was twenty-seven, and 69 percent of them were mulattos (versus only one-quarter of the total black population) at a time when lighter skin meant higher social status. Most of them were artisans or petty proprietors, clerks, teachers, and other low white-collar workers. Although they lived among their poorer black brethren near the waterfront or in the city's seventh ward, they were in a social class apart from most of their neighbors. The *Sunday Mercury* described them as "a well-behaved, gentlemanly set of young fellows." As an elite black sports association, the Pythian club provided its members with recreation and a means of displaying their privileged social status. Many of them were active in black social and civic organizations, and almost half belonged to the Banneker Institute, a literary and debating society that shared a room with the baseball players. One-fifth of these athletes also joined civil rights organizations, such as the Pennsylvania State Equal Rights League and the Social, Civil, and Statistical Association of the Colored People of Pennsylvania. A small minority of activists were members of a committee to recruit blacks for the Union army in 1863.

While most of their fellow African Americans suffered from poverty and racism, the Pythians had the leisure time and money to play baseball. A significant number of them also worked to improve the status of blacks in Philadelphia. Yet they also had a few critics in the black community who questioned the appropriateness of organized recreation such as baseball during the years of trial for northern blacks and recently emancipated southern slaves. William Still, a coal dealer, was a former fugitive slave and a leader of Philadelphia's Vigilance Association who was one of the key activists in the Underground Railroad between Washington and Canada. In 1869 he scolded the Pythians after he received a bill for dues owed to that club. In 1869 he wrote in reply: "Our kin in the South famishing for knowledge, have claims so great and pressing that I feel bound to give of any means in this direction to the extent of my abilities, in preference to giving for frivolous amusements. Again the poor are all around us in great want, whose claims I consider cannot be wholly ignored without doing violence to the Spirit of Christianity and humanity. At all events it seems to accord more fully with my idea of duty to give where it will do the most good, and where the greatest needs are manifest." The club secretary, Jacob C. White, Jr., responded by claiming that Still had in fact agreed to become a contributing member. He refused to comment on Still's priorities and again requested that Still pay his debt, adding: "neither the acquisition nor the disposition of your means is a matter of interest to us as an organization; we have nothing to say with reference to your giving to 'Our kin famishing for Knowledge or the suffering poor around us.' "

White and Octavius V. Catto were mulatto members of the Pythians who became leaders of Philadelphia's black community during the Reconstruction era. White, the son of a successful real estate agent and merchant, was a prominent abolitionist and activist prior to the war. He also promoted selective black emigration to Haiti. He made his greatest mark in the field of education, serving from 1864 until 1896 as the principal of the largest and most advanced black public school in his city. While he remained active in several civic and civil rights associations, he was a moderate on race questions, steadily pursuing a policy of accommodation with whites.

In 1867 the Pythians chose Catto as the field captain of their first nine for their first full season of interclub matches. Twenty-eight years old, he was viewed as a smart field general and strong player who worked with White to expand the club's schedule, recruit talented athletes, and fight for acceptance by the white baseball fraternity. Over the next few years Catto also labored off the field for civil rights for African-Americans in Philadelphia, including the integration of the city's streetcars and the right to vote. The passage of the Fifteenth Amendment that gave blacks the right to vote in 1870 raised tensions in Philadelphia. In October of 1871 Democratic politicians incited a crowd of Irish residents to attack the newly enfranchised black voters. An Irishman named Frank Kelly shot and killed Catto, who was honored with a procession down Broad Street and a full military funeral. The *Philadelphia Bulletin* eulogized him as "a good citizen, a pure and honest man, a ripe scholar and a consistent friend of the oppressed negroes." Kelly was arraigned six years later, but was never convicted.

The Pythians and a few other African-American clubs emulated the white associations in their charters and rules, social life, match play, intercity tours, and competition for state and national black championships. The Pythians issued and received formal challenges to compete against rivals from Camden (NJ), West Chester and Harrisburg (PA), Washington, D.C., and Brooklyn. Like their white counterparts, they sometimes entertained their guests at lavish dinners. Their great success on the ball field was due in part to recruiting outsiders to bolster their first nines for special matches, just as many white clubs did, even though this was in violation of NABBP rules.

In the summer of 1867 the Pythians played a series of matches against two black nines from Washington, D.C.—the Alerts and the Mutuals. They split the first set in July in Philadelphia, but swept both games from their rivals in the nation's capital in late August. A highlight of their contest against the Alerts in Washington was the attendance of the former abolitionist and Republican activist Frederick Douglass. His son Charles, third baseman for the Alerts, had spent three years with the Freedmen's Bureau before securing a position as a clerk in the Treasury department. Correspondence in the records of the Pythians suggests that a few other members of the Alerts and Mutuals were also employees of the federal government.

Black clubs sometimes also displayed the animosity and contentiousness exhibited by white organizations. When the Philadelphia Excelsiors challenged the Uniques of Williamsburgh (Brooklyn) for the black championship of the United States in the fall of 1867, their chaotic contest went from bad to worse. According to *Wilkes' Spirit*, "wrangling, disputing, bullying, charging, denying, cursing, and countering from first to last were the order of the meeting," At 5:30 P.M., with the Brooklyn club at bat and likely to win, the Excelsiors "profited by the examples set them by their white brothers, declared that it was too 'dark' to continue the game, and the umpire called it and awarded the ball to the Philadelphians." Only police intervention prevented the ensuing tumult from turning into a full-scale riot.

During the late 1860s the issues of equal opportunity and racial harmony naturally attracted much attention in the nation, especially in eastern cities where the rage for baseball was most intense. In general the leading black baseball clubs of Brooklyn, Newark, Philadelphia, and Washington, D.C., were on good terms with white organizations and frequently obtained permission to use their grounds for feature contests. White umpires sometimes even officiated at blacks' games. The Pythians enjoyed harmonious ties with the Athletics, who were generous with their facilities and support. In 1868 the Pythians' secretary, Jacob C. White, Jr., congratulated the Athletics after a "brilliant victory" that upheld "the pride of Philadelphia on the base-ball field." The secretary of the Athletics thanked White for "these manifestations of confidence from our brethren in the city, that have met with us on all sides."

Although white and black baseball players generally got along well, there was still much resistance among the white fraternity to the recognition of equality inherent in interracial competition. This opposition was overcome to some degree in Philadelphia in September 1869, thanks to the efforts of Col. Thomas Fitzgerald, a former president of the Athletics and editor of a local newspaper, the *City Item*. According to *Wilkes' Spirit*, while the Athletics "would have naught to do with the dusky votaries of the bat and ball," Fitzgerald did manage to arrange a match between the Olympics of Philadelphia and the Pythians (who prepared for the historic encounter by recruiting outsiders from New Jersey). The Olympics defeated the Pythians, 44–23, in front of a large crowd attracted by the novelty of the match. *Wilkes' Spirit* praised the experiment, declaring that "old-time prejudices are melting away in this country." It noted that interracial sporting contests were common in England and other countries and added: "It is not considered outside our own territory a lessening of dignity nor in the least disparaging to white men that they contend with blacks." It was hoped that "now the prejudice has been broken through here, it will be entirely swept away." A few weeks later the Pythians did defeat a white nine fielded by Fitzgerald's newspaper, 27–17, at the Athletics' ball field. Also in September the Olympics of Washington, D.C. manhandled the black Alerts of that city on the grounds of the Nationals, 56–4, in front of a large assembly of men and women of both races, as well as many government officials. In late September of 1870 a white club and a black club in Boston—each called the Resolutes—competed for the right to keep that name. The "colored" Resolutes triumphed, 25–15. According to the *Clipper*, it was a victory for the "son of Hams, who 'fought nobly' for their cherished title, out-playing their fair-faced friends at every point of the game, especially in the field."

While African-American nines had some success in persuading white teams to compete with them on the nation's diamonds, either in local matches or on more extended tours, they were excluded from tournaments and also membership in national and state associations. The organizers of an 1870 Chicago amateur competition barred that city's Blue Stockings, a black club. The Blue Stockings' secretary speculated that his team was denied the chance to play because the white clubs were afraid "of us beating them." However, the *Chicago Tribune* maintained that officials had rejected the team because it was considered too weak to be competitive with the white nines. The *Tribune* did concede that "probably their social standing had somewhat to do with the matter." It pointed out that Chicago's white amateur clubs included young men from some of the best families in the city who "were not disposed to burlesque the tournament by the admission of a colored club of inferior capacity, even though the gate receipts should suffer thereby."

The national and state baseball associations tried to enlist large numbers of white clubs while they banned black nines that were eager to join. Although the latter often shared playing fields and enjoyed good relations with white teams, they were denied equal representation in baseball gatherings, as they were excluded from Reconstruction-era politics in the North. The 1867 NABBP convention flatly refused to admit clubs with black delegates. Its Nominating Committee reported: "If colored clubs were admitted there would be in all probability some division of feeling, whereas, by excluding them no injury could result to anybody, and the possibility of any rupture being created on political grounds would be avoided." State meetings followed the same segregationist policy. The Pythians sent an emissary to Harrisburg in 1867 to present the club's credentials to the Pennsylvania gathering, but he found that only a few friends from the Athletics and other clubs favored admitting his club. Supporters advised a discrete withdrawal to avoid humiliation, and the Pythian delegate reluctantly finally concurred. "Whilst all expressed sympathy for our club," he reported, "a few only . . . expressed a willingness to vote for our admission, while numbers of the others openly said that they would in justice to the opinion of the clubs they represented be compelled, tho against their personal feelings, to vote against our admission." He was treated with courtesy and respect, receiving an invitation to attend an afternoon game and a free railroad pass home, but his club was not welcome in his state association. Similarly, the New York state association approved a motion in 1870 that if any of the clubs admitted were found to be composed of gentlemen of color, their association membership would be voided. The *Clipper* objected, stating (inaccurately): "Thus, for the first time in the history of the National Association, was a political question introduced as a bone of contention in the council of fraternity." That paper later advised black clubs to organize "a National Association of their own." Yet despite these snubs and setbacks, black baseball continue to grow during the Reconstruction era.

Baseball's trials and triumphs on both the battlefront and the home front during the Civil War contributed greatly to its impressive postwar boom after 1865. The central issues of the war—nationalism and Union versus states rights and secession, and the future of slavery and race relations—also had profound implications for the fate of baseball, and influenced its prospects for becoming the true national pastime for all regions and peoples of the United States. Civilians and former soldiers in the conflict both contributed greatly to the growth of the sport in the South and West after the return of peace. African-Americans founded clubs and challenged white players to treat them as equals on America's ball fields. While they achieved some small gains in the use of facilities owned by white clubs, and played in a few interracial matches, black players and clubs were barred from state and national baseball associations and tournament and championship matches. By the end of the 1860s baseball was well on its way to becoming popular across the continent, but more than three-quarters of a century would pass before full desegregation would even begin in the United States.

Epilogue

M odern baseball was in its infancy when the Civil War began, and the four years of murderous combat profoundly shaped the sport that was struggling to establish itself as the national pastime of the United States. During the late 1850s and 1860s the version of the game created in the New York City region and adopted by the National Association of Base Ball Players defeated rival forms of ball play and planted itself in all regions of the country. Prior to Fort Sumter some journalists were already honoring it with the title of "national game." During the war it strengthened its ties to American nationalism through informal matches contested in both Union and Confederate army and prison camps. After the return of peace, baseball became a means of sectional reconciliation between North and South. It expanded its connection with nationalism through imperialist ventures, new wars, and patriotic myths and rituals. It also associated itself with democratic traditions of equal opportunity and the assimilation of immigrants (but not yet African-Americans) into the mainstream of American society.

Prior to 1861 the New York City brand of baseball invented by the Knickerbocker Base Ball Club in the 1840s was well on its way to regional dominance in the Northeast, and it had already made inroads into the West and the South. Personal contacts, intercity tours, publicity provided by sporting weekly magazines published in Manhattan, and the work of the sport's first governing body—the National Association of Base Ball Players—all contributed mightily to the dominance of the game from Gotham over cricket and forms of townball popular in other regions. The "New

York game" triumphed in part because players and spectators favored its rules, but also because it was a product of the city that was the business, transportation, and media capital of the United States. New Yorkers exported and promoted their native sport as the American national pastime. They knew that they had an entertaining athletic recreation, and they marketed it extremely well.

When the Civil War began in April 1861 the fighting transformed all areas of American life, including of course athletic sports. The widespread familiarity with a variety of forms of baseball in all regions guaranteed that it would become a feature of military life for both sides of the conflict. While some commentators pondered the analogy between team sports and battle, ball players who enlisted as soldiers competed on makeshift playing fields. Within a few years Confederate and Union prisoners of war were even enjoying the game during their time of incarceration. Scattered evidence suggests that these matches played in army and prison camps did ultimately help to popularize the sport in all regions, with the "New York game" the main beneficiary.

The war naturally disrupted baseball on the home front, as many players enlisted and several clubs either disbanded or curtailed operations—especially during 1861 and 1862. But for those enthusiasts who avoided or evaded military service, the last two years of the conflict witnessed impressive growth and substantial changes in the sport. City championship matches and intercity tours generated real excitement during that period, most impressively in the major cities of the northeast. Entrepreneurs in Brooklyn inaugurated the commercialization of the sport that would grow into a small business within a decade. Manhattan and Brooklyn continued to lead the baseball world, but the explosive growth of the game in Philadelphia was noteworthy. Moreover, during this period the National Association modified the rules of the game, especially concerning pitching regulations. Club officials also acknowledged the horrendous carnage on the battlefields, and scheduled benefit contests to raise funds for injured soldiers. It is striking that during such a time of national calamity amusements in general and baseball in particular thrived in many communities.

During the Civil War thousands of civilians of both sexes and from diverse social, ethnic, and racial backgrounds played or watched ball games. The vast majority were boys and young men of humble or moderate means who arranged informal matches for fun. College students enrolled at Princeton, Harvard, and other institutions joined in the action. African-Americans began participating and struggled for equal opportunity to compete with whites. Journalists and club officials encouraged women to attend games to lend greater respectability to the new sport and to help control unruly males. The most talented adults competed in featured championship matches. At the highest level of play the advent of commercialism and professionalism generated some disturbing trends, including ill will among clubs, gambling, and charges of corruption. Social and political factionalism among club followers contributed to a few nasty incidents and spectator disorders.

The postwar baseball boom of the late 1860s had a significant impact on the process and central issues of Reconstruction. As army veterans spread the gospel of baseball in all regions after the war, many northern club officials used intercity tours to the West and the South as a means of sectional reconciliation. Others who enjoyed baseball prior to the war but who never served in the military relocated after the conflict and helped to promote the game in their adopted communities. Apart from the momentous question of reunion, the other central issue of this period concerned race relations and the prospects for equality for African-Americans. After 1865 black participation in the national pastime increased dramatically, but they were excluded from white clubs and state and national associations. While there were a few interracial contests, African-Americans were barred from full participation in baseball immediately after the Civil War. Except for a few places in professional leagues in the late 1880s, they would remain outside of the mainstream of American baseball until the mid-twentieth century.

After 1870 the ties between baseball and American nationalism would grow stronger as the nation flexed its muscles in the international arena. Waves of imperialism and new wars would present renewed opportunities for Americans to use the national pastime to promote American interests abroad—especially in the Caribbean and the Far East. Ball playing missionaries, diplomats, businessmen, soldiers, and sailors would teach the game to foreigners as they championed the American way of life. Executives and players from Major League Baseball would conduct world tours to showcase the excellence of baseball for disbelieving peoples around the globe. At home and overseas, enlisted men would play baseball to demonstrate their loyalty to their flag and their nation.

Patriotic myths and rituals would reinforce these connections between baseball and Americanism. The Doubleday-Cooperstown story linked the sport to a Civil War general. In addition, after Abraham Lincoln's assassination countless journalists, biographers, and historians elevated his reputation to heroic and legendary proportions. As they did so, it was only natural that they found ways to tie his name to the national pastime. While there is precious little hard evidence proving that Lincoln actually played, watched, or even paid attention to baseball, nevertheless there are several tales that connect him to the sport. Certainly as president, Lincoln had ample opportunity to see a baseball game. Before, during, and after the war baseball clubs competed on the President's Grounds near the White House in Washington, D.C. In June 1865, just two months after his assassination, the *New York Herald* announced that a feature match would be played there in August between the Atlantics of Brooklyn and the Athletics of Philadelphia. That journal added that the slain president had "expressed a wish to see a game of the kind." Albert G. Spalding also contributed to the folklore of Lincoln and baseball. A few years after spinning his yarn about Doubleday and Cooperstown, Spalding claimed that he had received a letter describing the visit of a Republican committee that traveled to Springfield, Illinois to notify Lincoln of his selection as the party's nominee for the presidency. According to Spalding, the men found him "engaged in a game of Base Ball." When a messenger alerted him to the imminent arrival of the delegation, he replied: "Tell the gentlemen that I am glad to know of their coming; but they'll have to wait a few minutes until I make another base hit."

Other stories come from the pens of Winfield Scott Larner and Frank B. Blair. Larner, a resident of Washington, wrote his account fifty years after a game played in the nation's capital. According to him, Lincoln and his son Tad watched the contest from a spot along the first base line, cheering with their fellow fans and also receiving an ovation from the crowd. Perhaps a more reliable account of Lincoln's love of baseball appears in Blair's 'Abe' Lincoln's Yarns and Stories. He remembered that as a boy during the Civil War he and his friends would visit his grandfather's estate in Silver Springs, Maryland. Lincoln made frequent trips to the Blair house, and Blair recalled that during these excursions Lincoln loved to play town ball with the youngsters on the lawn. "I remember vividly," Blair wrote, "how he ran with the children; how long were his strides, and how far his coat-tails stuck out behind, and how we tried to hit him with the ball, as he ran the bases. He entered into the spirit of the play as completely as any of us, and we invariably hailed his coming with delight." If Lincoln did have any experience with baseball prior to his election as president it was most likely with premodern versions of town ball. Perhaps each of these stories has some element of truth. More importantly, they demonstrate the power of both the Lincoln legend and the mythology of baseball—both expressions of American nationalism.

The playing of the national anthem during games (begun near the end of World War One in the 1918 World Series) and the tradition of the President throwing out the first ball on opening day intensified the association between the sport and American nationalism. More recently, ceremonies on baseball diamonds that honored the victims and heroes of the terrorist attack on the United States on September 11, 2001, also made this connection. Myths of equal opportunity and assimilation of immigrants and minorities would also enhance these links, as outsiders struggled to gain acceptance into the mainstream of American society through baseball. The ties between baseball and the American nation first forged in the Civil War continue into the twenty-first century.

Bibliographical Essay

The most detailed accounts of early baseball in the United States appear in the first sporting weekly periodicals, especially *Porter's Spirit of the Times*, *Wilkes' Spirit of the Times*, *The New York Clipper*, and the *Ball Players' Chronicle*. A few daily newspapers and weekly magazines printed occasional articles about major matches and important developments. Among these the most extensive coverage may be found in the *Brooklyn Daily Eagle*. Others with useful information for this project include the *Charleston Mercury* (SC), *Harper's Weekly*, the *New York Times*, the *New York Herald*, the *New York Sunday Mercury*, the *Newark Daily Advertiser*, the *Philadelphia Inquirer*, the *Philadelphia Sunday Dispatch*, and the *Philadelphia Sunday Mercury*. For personal reminiscences, see James D'Wolf Lovett, *Old Boston Boys and the Games They Played* (Boston, 1907). There is also a wealth of primary source materials in the Henry Chadwick scrapbooks in the Albert G. Spalding collection in the New York Public Library. For Princeton's baseball team, see the college's *Nassau Literary Magazine*, XXIII (March 1863), 282, and XXIV (September 1863), 48.

Many Civil War diaries and regimental histories include brief references to amusements in general and ball playing in particular among Union and Confederate soldiers. Those quoted in this book include Lemuel A. Abbott, *Personal Recollections and Civil War Diary, 1864* (Burlington, VT, 1908), 13, 20, 27–28, 41; John G. B. Adams, *Reminiscences of the Nineteenth Massachusetts Regiment* (Boston, 1899), 60–61; Thomas M. Aldrich, *The History of Battery A, First Regiment Rhode Island Light Artillery, in the War to Preserve the Union, 1861–65* (Providence, RI, 1904), 273–75; William Bates, *The Stars and Stripes in Rebeldom* (Boston, 1862), 127; Jacob H. Cole, *Under Five Commanders, or a Boy's Experience with the Army of the Potomac* (Paterson, NJ, 1906), 28; William J. Crossly, *Personal Narratives of Events in the*

War of the Rebellion, Sixth Series, No. 4 (Providence RI, 1903), 43–44; Charles E. Davis, Jr., *Three Years in the Army: The Story of the Thirteenth Massachusetts Volunteers, from July 16, 1861 to August 1, 1864* (Boston, 1894), 56; Dr. R. Hundley, *Prison Echoes of the Great Rebellion* (New York, 1874), 120, 135; George Lewis, *History of Battery E, First Regiment Rhode Island Light Artillery* (Providence, RI, 1892), 26; Adolphus W. Magnum, "Salisbury Prison," in Walter Clark, ed., *Histories of the Several Regiments and Battalions from North Carolina in the Great War, 1861–65*, 5 vols. (Raleigh, NC: The State of North Carolina, 1901), IV, 747; Lt. M. McNamara, "Lieutenant Charlie Pierce's Daring Attempts to Escape from Johnson's Island," *Southern Historical Society Papers*, VIII (January 1880), 62–63; Lt. William Peel, excerpts from his diary in "The Game Endures: A Civil War Diary," *Humanities*, Vol. 15, No 4 (July/August 1994), 18; George H. Putnam, *Memories of My Youth, 1844–1865* (New York, 1914), 304–306; George T. Stevens, *Three Years in the Sixth Corps, 77th Regiment, New York Volunteers*, 2nd ed. (New York, 1870), 84, 183; Mason Whiting Tyler, *Recollections of the Civil War* (New York, 1912), 78.

For secondary sources on early baseball see Melvin L. Adelman, *A Sporting Time: New York City and the Rise of Modern Athletics, 1820–70* (Urbana, Illinois, 1986), and "The First Baseball Game, the First Newspaper References to Baseball, and the New York Club. A Note on the Early History of Baseball," *Journal of Sport History* 7 (Winter 1980), 132–35; John A. Blanchard, *The H Book of Harvard Athletics, 1852–1922* (Cambridge, MA, 1923), 150–57; John M. Carroll, "The Doubleday Myth and Texas Baseball," *Southwestern Historical Quarterly* XCII (April 1989), 596–612; Jerrold Casway, "Philadelphia's Pythians," *The National Pastime*, No. 15 (1995), 120–23; W. Harrison Daniel, "The Rage in the Hill City: The Beginnings of Baseball in Lynchburg," *Virginia Cavalcade* XXVIII (Spring 1979): 186–91; Warren Goldstein, *Playing for Keeps: A History of Early Baseball* (Ithaca, N.Y., 1989); Stephen Jay Gould, "The Creation Myths of Cooperstown," *Natural History* (November 1989), 14–24; Kenneth S. Greenberg, *Honor and Slavery* (Princeton, NJ, 1996), 115–24; Robert W. Henderson, "How Baseball Began," *New York Public Library Bulletin*, 41 (April 1937), 287–91, and "Baseball and Rounders," *New York Public Library Bulletin*, 43 (April 1939), 303–14; Frederick Ivor-Campbell, Robert L. Tiemann, and Mark

Rucker, eds., *Baseball's First Stars* (Cleveland, OH, 1996); George B. Kirsch, *The Creation of American Team Sports: Baseball and Cricket, 1838–72* (Urbana, Illinois, 1989), and "Baseball Spectators, 1855–1870," *Baseball History* 1 (Fall 1987), 4–20; Peter Levine, A.G. *Spalding and the Rise of Baseball: The Promise of American Sport* (New York, 1985); Tom Melville, *Early Baseball and the Rise of the National League* (Jefferson, NC, 2001); Patricia Millen, *From Pastime to Passion: Baseball and the Civil War* (Bowie, MD, 2001); Harold Peterson, *The Man Who Invented Baseball* (New York, 1969); Frank Presbrey, *Athletics at Princeton: A History* (New York, 1901), 20–27, 67–87; Francis C. Richter, *The History and Early Records of Base Ball* (Philadelphia, 1914); William J. Ryczek, *When Johnny Came Sliding Home: The Post-Civil War Baseball Boom, 1865–1870* (Jefferson, NC, 1998); Harold Seymour, *Baseball: the Early Years* (New York, 1960), and "How Baseball Began," *New York Historical Society Quarterly* 40 (October 1956), 369–85; Duane A. Smith, "Dickey Pearce: Baseball's First Great Shortstop," *National Pastime*, No. 10 (1990), 38–42; Albert Spalding, *America's National Game* (New York, 1911); James L. Terry, *Long Before the Dodgers: Baseball in Brooklyn, 1855–1884* (Jefferson, NC, 2002); Robert L. Tiemann and Mark Rucker, eds., *Nineteenth Century Stars* (Kansas City, MO, 1989); Wells Twombly, *200 Years of Sport in America* (New York, 1976), 71; Jules Tygiel, *Past Time: Baseball as History* (New York, 2000), chapters 1, 2; Ian Tyrrell, "The Emergence of Modern American Baseball c. 1850–1880," in Richard Cashman and Michael McKernan, eds., *Sport in History: The Making of Modern Sport History* (Queensland, Australia, 1979), 205–26; David Q. Voigt, *American Baseball*, vol. 1 (Norman, OK, 1966).

The Civil War has generated a vast literature of secondary works, including several valuable books and articles on the experiences of soldiers. For general works of this type, see Larry M. Logue, *To Appomattox and Beyond: The Civil War Soldier in War and Peace* (Chicago, IL, 1996); Reid Mitchell, *Civil War Soldiers* (New York, 1988) and *The Vacant Chair: The Northern Soldier Leaves Home* (New York, 1993); James I. Robertson, Jr., *Soldiers Blue and Gray* (Columbia, SC, 1988); Bell Irvin Wiley, *The Life of Johnny Reb: The Common Soldier of the Confederacy* (Indianapolis, 1943) and *The Life of Billy Yank: The Common Soldier of the Union* (Indianapolis, 1952). On the prison camps, see Louis A. Brown, *The Salisbury Prison: A Case Study of Confederate Military Prisons, 1861–65* (Wendell, NC, 1980), 136–37; Phillip R. Shriver and Donald J. Breen, "Ohio's Military Prisons in the Civil War," (Ohio State University Press for the Ohio Historical Society, 1964), 36–37.

For articles on recreation and sports in general and baseball in particular in northern and southern army and prison camps see John R. Betts, "Home Front, Battle Field, and Sport during the Civil War," *Research Quarterly* 42 (May 1971), 127; David S. Crockett, "Sports and Recreational Practices of Union and Confederate Soldiers," *Research Quarterly* 32 (October 1961), 335–47; Lawrence W. Fielding, "Sport on the Road to Appomattox: The Shadows of Army Life" (Unpublished Ph.D. dissertation, University of Maryland, 1974); "Sport and the Terrible Swift Sword," *Research Quarterly* 48 (March 1977), 1–11; "War and the Trifles: Sport in the Shadows of Civil War Army Life," *Journal of Sport History* 4 (1977), 151–68; Jim Sumner, "Baseball at Salisbury Prison Camp," *Baseball History*, 1ˢᵗ ed. (Westport CT, 1989), 19–27.

Index